THE APOCRITICUS OF
MACARIUS MAGNES

THE APOCRITICUS OF MACARIUS MAGNES

By T·W·CRAFER, D·D.

WIPF & STOCK · Eugene, Oregon

Wipf and Stock Publishers
199 W 8th Ave, Suite 3
Eugene, OR 97401

The Apocriticus of Macarius Magnes
By Crafer, T. W.
Softcover ISBN-13: 979-8-3852-0935-4
Hardcover ISBN-13: 979-8-3852-0936-1
eBook ISBN-13: 979-8-3852-0937-8
Publication date 12/6/2023
Previously published by SPCK, 1919

This edition is a scanned facsimile of the original edition published in 1919.

CONTENTS

INTRODUCTION :—

	PAGE
Summary	ix
The Nature of the *Apocriticus*	x
The History of the *Apocriticus* to 1867	xi
Its History since 1867	xii
The Heathen Objections in the *Apocriticus*	xiv
The Date of the *Apocriticus*	xvi
The Authorship of the *Apocriticus*	xix
The Title of the Work	xxiv
The Literary Relations of the *Apocriticus*	xxv
The Text and MSS.	xxvii
Its Theological and Apologetic Value	xxix

TRANSLATION :—

BOOK I. Fragment of ch. vi. Concerning Berenice or the woman with an issue of blood . . . 31

BOOK II. Ch. vii. Answer concerning the saying: Think not that I am come to send peace on the earth 32

Ch. viii. Answer concerning the saying: Who is my mother, who are my brethren? . . . 33

Ch. ix. Answer concerning the sayings: None is good save one, even God; and A good man out of the good treasure of his heart bringeth forth that which is good . . . 34

Ch. x. Answer concerning the saying: Lord, have pity on my son, for he is lunatic . . . 36

Ch. xi. Answer concerning the saying: If I bear witness of myself, my witness is not true . . 37

Chs. xii. and xvii. Question and answer concerning the discrepancies of the Evangelists (with brief introductions to the next five questions and answers by the Philosopher and the Christian) . 38

Chs. xiii. and xviii. Question and answer concerning the saying: But when they came to Jesus, when they saw He was already dead, they brake not His legs 41

CONTENTS

Chs. xiv. and xix. Question and answer concerning the Resurrection of Christ and His manifestation. 43
Chs. xv. and xx. Question and answer concerning the saying: Now is the judgment of the world, now shall the prince of this world be cast outside 46
Chs xvi. and xxi. Question and answer concerning the saying: Ye cannot hear my word . . 48

(The summaries of Books III and IV are translated from the headings of the chapters in the Athens MS.)

BOOK III. These words are contained in the Third Book of the words of Answer to the Greeks.[1]

Proem (Introduction to seven attacks by the Philosopher) 51
The Christian (Introduction to his seven answers) 51
Chs. i. and viii. How Jesus endured to be crucified with insult 52
Chs. ii. and ix. How it is said: If it be possible, let the cup pass 57
Chs. iii. and x. How it is said: If ye believe Moses, ye would believe me 60
Chs. iv. and xi. What is the meaning of the swine and the demons? 62
Chs. v. and xii. What is the meaning of the saying: It is easier for a camel to go through a needle, than a rich man into the kingdom of God? . 69
Chs. vi. and xiii. How it is said: About the fourth watch of the night He came upon the sea. . 73
Chs. vii. and xiv. What is the meaning of: The poor ye have always, but me ye have not always? . 76
The Greek (Introduction to the next eight attacks) 78
Chs. xv. and xxiii. (With the Christian's Introduction to his eight answers.)
What is the meaning of: Except ye eat my flesh and drink my blood, ye have no life in you? . 78
Chs. xvi. and xxiv. How it is said: And if they drink any deadly thing, it shall not hurt them . 85
Chs. xvii. and xxv. What is the meaning of the grain of mustard seed? 88
Chs. xviii. and xxvi. How it is said: Cast thyself down 89

[1] τῶν ἀποκριτικῶν πρὸς Ἕλληνας λόγων. But the full title of the work is first given as *The Apocriticus or Monogenes to the Greeks of Macarius Magnes, concerning the questions and solutions in the Gospel.*

CONTENTS

	PAGE
Chs. **xix. xx.** and **xxvii.** What is the meaning of: Get thee behind me, Satan; and the address to Peter? What is the meaning of the seventy times seven?	91

(The beginning of another proposition from the Acts of the Apostles.)

Chs. **xxi.** and **xxviii.** How Peter killed Ananias and Sapphira.	95
Chs. **xxii.** and **xxix.** How Peter went forth when the prison was shut	97
Chs. **xxx.** and **xxxvii.** (With brief introductions to the next six questions and answers by the Greek and the Christian.) How Paul circumcised Timothy.	99
Chs. **xxxi.** and **xxxviii.** How Paul says he is a Roman, though he was not a Roman	102
Chs. **xxxii.** and **xxxix.** How it is said: No one goeth a warfare at his own charges	103
Chs. **xxxiii.** and **xl.** How it is said: He is a debtor to do the whole law	105
Chs. **xxxiv.** and **xli.** How it is said: The law entered, that the transgression might abound.	107
Chs. **xxxv.** and **xlii.** How it is said: I would not that ye should become partakers of demons	108
Chs. **xxxvi.** and **xliii.** How it is said: In the latter times some shall depart from the faith	113

BOOK IV. The following is contained in the Fourth Book of the words of Answer to the Greeks.[1]

Proem (Introduction to ten attacks by the Philosopher)	117
The Christian (Introduction to his answer in eight chapters).	117
Chs. **i.** and **xi.** Concerning how it is said: The fashion of this world passeth away	118
Chs. **ii.** and **xii.** How it is said: We which are alive shall be caught up in the clouds	121
Chs. **iii.** and **xiii.** How he says: The Gospel shall be preached in all the world	124
Chs. **iv.** and **xiv.** How the Lord speaks to Paul by a vision, and how it befell that Peter was crucified	126
Chs. **v.** and **xv.** What is the meaning of: Take heed, for many shall come saying, I am Christ?.	127

[1] The full title is again first given, in somewhat different form, as *The Apocriticus or Monogenes to the Greeks of Macarius Magnes, concerning the questions and answers in dispute in the New Testament.*

CONTENTS

	PAGE
Chs. vi., vii. and xvi.[1] What is the meaning of the judgmen: in the Apocrypha? How it is said: The heaven shall be rolled together as a scroll, and the stars shall fall as leaves.	129
Chs. viii., ix. and xvii.[1] What is the meaning of the leaven, the mustard seed, and the pearl? How it is said: Thou hast hid these things from the wise and prudent, and revealed them unto babes.	133
Chs. x. and xviii. What is the meaning of: They that are whole need not a physician, but they that are sick?	136
Chs. xix. and xxv. (With brief Introductions to the next six questions and answers by the Philosopher and the Christian.) What is the meaning of: But ye were washed, but ye were sanctified?	138
Chs. xx. and xxvi. What is the meaning of the Monarchy?	143
Chs. xxi. and xxvii. What is the meaning of the angels having immortality? What is the meaning of the tables being written with the finger of God?[2]	145
Chs. xxii. and xxviii. How the Godhead was made flesh in Mary and was born	149
Chs. xxiii. and xxix. How it is said: Thou shalt not revile gods	151
Chs. xxiv. and xxx. What is the meaning of the resurrection of the flesh?	153

BOOK V.

Fragment quoted in Greek by F. Turrianus in the sixteenth century	164
Further quotation from the same author, which is probably a translation of Macarius	165
INDEX .	167

[1] Macarius replies to two questions in one answer.
[2] The heading gives it thus as two separate chapters, although there is but one chapter in the text in the case of both question and answer.

NOTE.—When passages in the *Apocriticus* are referred to by page and line, the numbering is that of the Greek edition, and not of the translation contained in this book.

INTRODUCTION

An introduction to the *Apocriticus* of Macarius Magnes cannot be written on the ordinary lines. This is the first time that it has been introduced to English readers, and those who wish to study it in the original Greek will find it very difficult to obtain a copy of the only edition. My own study of this obscure and neglected author has probably been more lengthy than that of any one outside Germany, and it is therefore a great pleasure to share with others the result of it. He is still surrounded with so much uncertainty that it is impossible to offer final conclusions with regard to him, but he is full of an interest which is in many ways unique, and his work not only affords a critical problem which should prove fascinating to many besides myself, but also contains much that is both interesting and novel. The *Apocriticus* really presents us with two separate works, for the questions of a heathen objector are in each case quoted verbatim before the "answer" is given. As the objections represent an attack on the Scriptures in detail, and undoubtedly reflect the philosophy of Porphyry, the famous Neoplatonist of the third century, the reproduction of them preserves for us a form of anti-Christian literature in a fulness which has no parallel. I have therefore translated them without any abbreviation. The answers have proved too lengthy to give in full, but, rather than offer a mere selection, I have translated the most important parts, and given the rest in the form of a summary.

Such is the chequered history of the work, that the author's name, date, and country have always been a matter of doubt, while the dialogue which he claims to

x INTRODUCTION

be reproducing in his book has generally been considered a mere literary device. It was rescued from oblivion by its use in a bitter controversy in the ninth century, after which there is no mention of it until the sixteenth, when its use was again controversial. When its genuineness was then called in question, the only Manuscript was found to have disappeared from Venice. Nothing more is heard of the book until 1867, when a Manuscript was found in Epirus, and taken to Athens. It was collated by a young French scholar, who died before it could be published. The destructive criticism of a series of German scholars reduced its importance and checked the study of it. While I was myself talking of another collation, a German scholar sought it at Athens and found that the Manuscript was not in the Library, but in private possession, with the risk of being lost. The only edition is increasingly difficult to obtain, and there is a danger of the *Apocriticus* again sinking into oblivion. I therefore greatly welcome this opportunity of making it more widely known.

THE NATURE OF THE *APOCRITICUS*.

It may be stated at the outset that it was originally a work in five books, and claims to represent a dialogue between Macarius and a heathen philosopher, which took place on five successive days. The Athens MS. is mutilated, beginning in Chapter VII of Book II, and ending in the middle of Chapter XXX of Book IV. A fragment of Book I has been preserved in Nicephorus,[1] and I had myself the good fortune to discover a fragment of Book V in Turrianus.[2] The questions are mostly objections to selected verses of the Gospels, Acts, and Pauline Epistles, but one or two concern the Old Testament, and some in the later part are purely doctrinal. There seems some sequence in their subjects,

---

[1] See Nicephorus, *Antirrhetici Libri*, ap. Pitra, *Spicilegium Solesmense*, tom. i. p. 303 et seq.

[2] Turrianus, *Dogmaticus de Justificatione ad Germanos adversus Luteranos*, Romae, 1557, p. 37 et seq.

INTRODUCTION xi

Christ's miracles being first attacked, and then His words, the chief charge being that of inconsistency. There follow like charges of inconsistency against S. Peter and S. Paul, and then objections are brought to such doctrines as the Incarnation, the Monarchy of God, and the Resurrection. The fragment from Book V suggests that the latter part dealt with some of the more inward doctrines of Christianity, such as justification by faith.[1] The method of the book is to give about seven objections in a series, and then their respective answers, with a few words of introduction in each case, especially at the beginning of each book.

THE HISTORY OF THE *APOCRITICUS* TO 1867.

The book seems to have disappeared until the ninth century. This is not to be wondered at when the anti-Christian blasphemy of the questions is remembered, which might have caused its suppression under the edicts of Theodosius II or Justinian. Possibly the survival of the copy then brought to light was due to the fact that it had as frontispiece a portrait of the author in ecclesiastical vestments. In the Iconoclastic controversy, those who were in favour of the destruction of images garbled a quotation from it as a support to their position. Nicephorus, Patriarch of Constantinople, in answering them, had some difficulty in finding out anything about it. He was able to show that his opponents had used it wrongly, but regarded it with little favour on the ground that it was inclined towards heresy. His importance, however, lies in the fact that he also quoted a fragment from the first book, which has not been preserved otherwise. It contains part of the answer of Macarius to an objection to the miracle of the woman with the issue of blood, in which the story appears that she was a great woman of Edessa named Berenice, and that a bronze statue in that city still commemorated her healing.[2]

[1] See p. 166, n. 1.   [2] See p. 31.

xii INTRODUCTION

The *Apocriticus* next appears in the sixteenth century, when it was one of the favourite weapons in the patristic armoury of the Jesuit Franciscus Turrianus (De la Torre) in his controversy with the Lutherans.[1] He not only quotes from all the extant books, but makes a quotation from the lost fifth book. He gives the author's name as Magnetes, and places his date soon after A.D. 150. His opponents in the Eucharistic controversy refused to believe that there was such a book, and when search was made in S. Mark's Library at Venice, the MS. was nowhere to be found, though mentioned in the catalogue. Little is heard about the book in the centuries that followed. Boivin, of Paris, considered the author to have been a younger contemporary of Athanasius. Magnus Crusius,[2] a Göttingen professor, believed his opponent to be none other than Porphyry the Neoplatonist, and placed the work at the end of the third or beginning of the fourth century. He held that neither of the author's appellations was necessarily his proper name, as of course Macarius Magnes may simply mean "The Blessed Magnesian."

ITS HISTORY SINCE 1867.

In 1867 a MS. of the *Apocriticus* was discovered at Athens, and on the death of its first editor, C. Blondel, it was finally published by his friend Foucart,[3] but without an introduction. This was supplied the next year by Duchesne,[4] who believed that the Athens MS. was identical with the one lost three centuries before at Venice. As other evidence has been added since his time, this theory cannot now be accepted. He thinks

[1] See F. Turrianus, *Adversus Magdeburgenses*, Colon. 1573, ii. 3, p. 165; i. 5, p. 21, and ii. 13, p. 208.
[2] See Migne, *Patr. Graec.* x. p. 1343 et seq. His opinions are summarised by Pitra, *Spicil. Solesm.* i. p. 545.
[3] *Macarii Magnetis quae supersunt, ex inedito codice edidit*, C. Blondel, Klincksieck, Paris, 1876. It is this which has been used in the translation which follows, and reference is occasionally made to its pages.
[4] *De Macario Magnete et scriptis ejus*, Klincksieck, Paris, 1877.

INTRODUCTION xiii

the author was from Magnesia, but locates his abode as near Edessa, giving him a date between A.D. 300 and 350. Concerning his opponent he makes the brilliant suggestion that he was the well-known Hierocles, who was something of a Neoplatonist philosopher, and a follower of Porphyry, but was also governor of Bithynia, and perhaps also at another time of Palmyra. This man wrote two books called *Philaletheis Logoi* (often simply referred to as *Philalethes*, or "Friend of truth"), and after addressing them "not against the Christians but to them,"[1] he became an instigator of the terrible persecution of the Christians which broke out under Diocletian in A.D. 303. I have found much to substantiate this theory, and shall therefore refer again to its acceptance.

However, a series of German critics[2] refused to date the work from the fourth century, and identified the author with the Macarius, Bishop of Magnesia, who was at the Synod of the Oak in A.D. 403, and accused Heraclides of Ephesus of heresy in his following of Origen. This new German theory was really an old French one, which had been suggested by Le Quien nearly two centuries before. There is much to be said against it, as I have shown in my articles on this subject in the *Journal of Theological Studies*.[3] It is quite impossible to repeat in this short introduction the arguments on this and many points, so I venture to refer the reader to what I have already written elsewhere. In 1911 Harnack took up the subject, and set forth lengthy arguments for the theory that the heathen objector is Porphyry himself, and actually suggested that it affords material for an edition of his lost treatise in fifteen books against

[1] Lactantius, *Div. Instit.* v. 2.
[2] Möller, *Schürer's Theol. Lit. Zeit.* 1877, p. 521; Zahn, *Zeitschrift für Kirchengeschichte*, B. ii. p. 450 et seq., 1878; Wagenmann, *Jahrbücher für Deutsche Theol.* B. xxii. p. 141, 1878. On such authority, Dr. Salmon simply states it as a fact in the article on Macarius in the *Dict. Christ. Biog.*
[3] See *J.T.S.* of April 1907 (vol. viii. No. 31), p. 404 et seq., *Macarius Magnes, a Neglected Apologist*, and July 1907 (vol. viii. No. 32, p. 546 et seq.).

xiv INTRODUCTION

the Christians.[1] But he has to admit that in any case the *Apocriticus* simply contains a series of excerpts from Porphyry made by a later anonymous writer, and that Macarius did not know they were from Porphyry, or he would not in one of his answers have referred his opponent to Porphyry's book *De Abstinentia* as an authority. With regard to the answers, Harnack accepts the theory of a later date, and puts aside my arguments in favour of the earlier. For the many weaknesses in his theory, and the difficulties which may be better overcome by other explanations, I must again refer to what I have already written.[2] The only other recent contribution to the subject was made by Schalkhausser,[3] who searched for the solitary MS. of the *Apocriticus* in the National Library at Athens, and made the strange discovery that the MS. had been the property of the late librarian Apostolides, who had left it to his widow, and it was now not to be traced. It may be mentioned here that ten short fragments remain of another work of Macarius, his Homilies on Genesis. The only place where they are all to be found together is an appendix to the treatise of Duchesne.[4] They contain the word Monogenes, which is the sub-title of the *Apocriticus*, as a title of God the Son. And the allegorical method used, including the interpretation of the coats of skins, shows the same following of Origen as we see in the rest of Macarius.

THE HEATHEN OBJECTIONS IN THE *APOCRITICUS*.

Nowhere else does so detailed an attack on Christianity remain to us. It evidently comes from one who is not merely engaged in the vulgar work of trying to destroy the faith; for he claims a higher morality, and writes as

[1] Kritik des Neues Testaments von einen griechischen Philosophen der 3 Jahrhunderts, etc. (*Texte und Untersuchungen*, etc. xxxvii. 4, Leipzig, 1911).
[2] *J.T.S.* April and July 1914 (vol. xv. Nos. 59 and 60), *The work of Porphyry against the Christians, and its reconstruction*.
[3] Georg Schalkhausser, *Zu der Schriften des Makarios von Magnesia*, Leipzig, 1907.
[4] *Op. cit.* pp. 39 and 12.

a philosopher. And the modern character of many of his attacks, and of some of his actual arguments, give his work more than an antiquarian interest. These assaults of long ago, which were successfully parried by a champion of the faith, may have a reassuring effect upon those who think that their religion has never met with such plausible assaults as to-day. They reflect the master-mind of Porphyry, the great Neoplatonist philosopher, but even Harnack admits that they are borrowed from him by some smaller man, who thus popularised his work. This is exactly the case of so many who speak and write against the Church to-day. And the most recent tendency of those who refuse to accept the Christian faith is to approve at least in some sense of its Founder Himself, but deny that the Church has either the power or the right to interpret Him to the world. The objections before us are mostly to the human side of the faith, and are directed against the Evangelists rather than the Leader whose words and deeds they profess to recount, and against the unreasonableness of the Apostles and their teaching rather than that of Christ.

We will take the theory as substantiated that the author was Hierocles, who attacked Christianity with the pen before he tried to destroy it with the sword of persecution. Harnack has given unintentional support by showing that the *Apocriticus* is really to be divided into two parts, after iii. 19, though the author has concealed the division.[1] This is a new argument for the theory that he is using the two books of the *Philaletheis Logoi*, or *Philalethes*, of Hierocles. But there are other problems connected with the *Apocriticus* which this theory helps to solve. For instance, Duchesne adduces an inscription[2] as proving that, before his governorship of Bithynia in A.D. 304 he had been in office at Palmyra. Now Macarius came from Asia Minor, but when he points his opponent to the effects of the faith, it is to Syria that he turns, especially to Edessa and Antioch.

[1] See p. 95, n. 2.
[2] *Corpus Inscript. Lat.* t. 3, No. 133, ap. Duch. p. 20.

xvi INTRODUCTION

Again, we find that in the *Apocriticus* the life of Christ is belittled by adducing that of Apollonius of Tyana, whose miracles were said to be superior, and who, instead of humbly submitting to death, "spoke boldly to the Emperor Domitian and then disappeared."[1] Eusebius himself wrote an answer to Hierocles, in which he says that Apollonius was thus adduced, and gives a statement of Philostratus about him, saying, "He says that he disappeared from the judgment-seat."[2] Lactantius gives similar testimony, for in writing about Hierocles he speaks of Apollonius "who, *as you describe*, suddenly was not to be found at the judgment-seat, when Domitian wished to punish him."[3] It may be added that, whereas the language of the objector in the *Apocriticus* has nothing in common with the extant words of Porphyry, there are a few sentences given by Eusebius[4] as occurring verbatim in the *Philalethes* of Hierocles, in which, out of eleven words of a distinctive kind, no less than seven are found in the *Apocriticus*.[5]

The Date of the *Apocriticus*.

Upon the date of Macarius depends the question as to whether a real dialogue underlies his work or not. If such is the case, we must place him at the beginning of the fourth century, though he may have written his book years after the dialogue had taken place. Critics have been so unanimous in declaring that the book was written long afterwards, and that its form is a mere literary device, that I do not like to make an assertion to the contrary. But at least I would plead that, unless other considerations make such a date impossible, there is a strong suggestion of reality about the dialogue described

[1] *Apocr.* iii. 1.
[2] Euseb., *In Hieroclem*, in Gottfriedus Alearius's edition of Philostratus, Lipsiae, 1709, p. 459. ἀφανισθῆναι φησὶν αὐτόν should be compared with ἀφανὴς ἐγένετο of the *Apocriticus*.
[3] *Div. Instit.* v. 3.
[4] Migne, *Patr. Graec.* xxii. pp. 797-800, ch. 2.
[5] For details, and for further points in this connexion, see *J.T.S.* of April 1911, p. 377 et seq.

INTRODUCTION xvii

as in process. For the questions as well as the answers sometimes contain indications of a dispute;[1] and a study of the author's remarks, made from time to time in the dialogue, shows him to have been either an unusually skilful simulator of doubts and fears which were not his, or a man giving a record of what had actually happened, though doubtless using the *book* into which Hierocles had already put the questions that he had raised in the debate. But, in any case, if Macarius is writing long after Christianity had ceased to be an unlawful religion, why should he adopt such a trembling attitude before his opponent, and need to brace himself continually against a nameless dread which nearly overwhelmed him? All is explained if it is reminiscent of a contest with a man who shortly afterwards became "prime mover in causing the persecution."[2] But this is not in the least like the language of Christians who faced opponents in later years. If the battle is only a literary one, and the Christian is showing, before a world in which the stigma of Christianity has been removed, how he got the upper hand, why should he cringe so before the heathen, as though he were making a desperate effort to uphold a humble and popular cause?[3] This was not the way to represent the relation of Christian and heathen a century later for the edification of fellow-Christians. If this be all literary padding, why is it of this kind?

A few suggested indications of date may now be added.

1. Twice it is stated that 300 years have passed since Christianity began.[4] But this is in the words of the heathen, not of Macarius, and in any case a round number does not count for much, especially in days before time was reckoned by the Christian era.

---

[1] e.g. *Apocr.* iii. 30, p. 125, l. 6, and iii. 36, p. 131, l. 9. It is argued that such remarks are merely interpolations, but sometimes (as in iv. 19) the personal introduction gradually shades off into the words of the objection.

[2] Lactantius, *De Mortibus Persecutorum*, xvi.

[3] See e.g. *Apocr.* ii. 12, and the Preface to iii. for the heathen's attitude, and iii. 10 for his own.

[4] *Apocr.* iv. 3, p. 160, l. 6, and iv. 5, p. 163, l 4.

B

xviii INTRODUCTION

2. In the other direction the date is limited by the statement that "many rule the world,"[1] and the taking of Hadrian as an example of a "monarch," for the Empire was divided among two Augusti and two Cæsars in the year A.D. 292.

3. Macarius gives a short list of some of the peoples of the earth who had not yet heard the preaching of the Gospel.[2] They not only include some of the Ethiopians, but also Mauretania, which had certainly heard the Gospel long before the end of the fourth century.

4. He also has a list of heretics, which does not extend further than the Manichæans, and makes no mention of the Arians. It is true that some have thought that the latter are meant by Christomachi (iii. 14, p. 91), but they are further defined as "sharers in Judaistic folly," and seem to refer to the Monarchians.

5. But in the eyes of all German critics other considerations have been considered enough to brush these aside. The Trinitarian doctrine of the book has been considered as belonging to a period some time after A.D. 325. It is true that there is a passage on the baptismal formula which contains the words "that the name of three Persons in one substance may be recognised."[3] But two points should be considered;[4]—this is not the ordinary use of the words ὑπόστασις and οὐσία in the book; and the whole passage is contained in twenty-three lines which are extraordinarily inappropriate to an argument with a pagan, with whom the argument has just been about the Monarchy of the one God. Brief theological phrases replace the usual diffuse style of Macarius, and the possibility is suggested that the words are a later interpolation, inserted for the instruction of Christians, not for the defence of the faith.

The other consideration is suggested by the likeness

[1] *Apocr.* ii. 15, p. 24.   [2] *Ibid.* iv. 13.
[3] *Ibid.* iv. 25: ἵνα τριῶν ὑποστάσεων ἐν οὐσίᾳ μιᾷ γνωισθῇ τὸ ὄνομα ; but this is not identical with the later stereotyped phrase μία οὐσία ἐν τρισὶν ὑποστάσεσιν.
[4] For a discussion of the whole subject, see *J.T.S.* of July 1907, p. 553 et seq. See also below, pp. xxviii, 141, 142, and 155.

INTRODUCTION xix

of some of the words and arguments of the *Apocriticus* to some of the fathers of the fourth century, notably Gregory of Nyssa. But an examination reveals the fact that the passages are mostly of a character which express ideas common in the fourth century, so that the theory that Macarius borrowed in each case cannot be substantiated. For instance, the language of Macarius about our Lord enticing the devil to attack Him in the Passion, and Satan, like a fish, gulping down the bait of His humanity, and so being caught by the hook of His divinity, is much like that of Gregory.[1] But a close parallel is found in a passage of Rufinus,[2] and another in Amphilochius.[3] And indeed the latter, in introducing it, uses the unusual title Monogenes in speaking of Christ; but this is the alternative title of the *Apocriticus* itself, and probably was originally the chief one. So that he may have used the title because he was borrowing from a book of that name. But as a matter of fact the simile dates back to Origen (*Comm. in Psalm* xxii.), and the idea is present in germ in Ignatius, *Ad. Eph.* xix.

For a further discussion of the date, I must refer to what I have written elsewhere.[4] If German conclusions are to be accepted, it is about A.D. 410. But sufficient has been said to show that there are many objections to this, and that it is quite possibly a century earlier. Of course this makes a great deal of difference to the importance of the answers.

THE AUTHORSHIP OF THE *APOCRITICUS*.

In spite of the ambiguity of his double name,[5] we may safely speak of the author as Macarius, and regard Magnes as a place-name, meaning "the Magnesian."

[1] *Apocr.* iii. 9; Greg. Nyss., *Or. Cat.* chs. xxi.-xxvi.
[2] Rufinus, *Comment. in Symb. Apost.* § 14.
[3] Holl., *Amphil.* p. 91 et seq.
[4] *J.T.S.* April and July 1907.
[5] Some scholars have regarded "The Blessed Magnesian" as simply a *nom de guerre*, or as suggesting an anonymous author, while others have simply written of him as Magnetes.

The question still remains whether the latter implies that he was Bishop of Magnesia. The fact that there was such a bishop, whose name was Macarius, has naturally suggested an identification of the two. Photius records that this Macarius came forward at the Synod of the Oak in A.D. 403 as one of those who accused Heraclides of Ephesus of heresy, his offence consisting of an undue following of Origen. But it is difficult to see how such a charge can have been brought by the author of the *Apocriticus*, who is himself steeped in Origenism. Not only was this the conclusion arrived at by Nicephorus, when he studied the book in the ninth century,[1] but it is obvious to any one who looks at it. And it is a complete puzzle why such a man should have thought it necessary to represent himself as having a desperate encounter with a heathen philosopher of a hundred years before, and facing his long-forgotten arguments in fear and trembling. And internal evidence is against the fact of the author having been a bishop. When his opponent says that, if to "drink any deadly thing" cannot hurt a true believer, this ought to be made a test in the choosing of bishops, there is no attempt at personal defence in the answer.[2] And, after giving examples of great bishops of former time and the power of their prayers, he refers to those of his own day in a way that seems to indicate that he himself bore no such exalted position in the Christian community. It is true that Nicephorus called him a "Hierarch," and said there was a portrait of him on the MS. of his book, in which he was robed as a priest,[3] but this does not prove anything.[4]

And it is evidently not in Asia Minor that the *Apocriticus* was written. It is not only that, as already

---

[1] He is condemned, particularly with regard to the non-eternity of punishment, of being a follower τοῦ δυσσεβοῦς καὶ ἀποπλήκτου 'Ωριγένους, Nic., *op. cit.*; cf. *Apocr.* iv. 16, p. 187, l. 32.

[2] *Apocr.* iii. 16, p. 96, and iii. 24, p. 108 et seq.

[3] Nic., *op. cit.*, στολὴν ἱερέως ἀμπεχόμενον.

[4] Lumper (ap. Migne, *Patr. Lat.* v. p. 343) suggests that our author was confused with the Macarius of the Oak, and "hinc fortasse sive fraude, sive ignorantia, Episcopi titulum addiderit librarius, Magnetis vetustioris opus exscribens."

INTRODUCTION xxi

stated,¹ he points his opponent to the East, and particularly to Antioch and Edessa, and that he once uses the Persian word "parasang" as a measure of distance.² But, when he gives a list of countries which had not yet heard the Gospel, he locates Ethiopia as south-*west*, which implies that he was as far eastward as Syria. And yet he shows a special interest in Asia Minor also. In his list of heretics, in which he refers exclusively to those of the East, he speaks of Montanus of Phrygia, and Dositheus of Cilicia, and he shows a knowledge of the Encratites of Asia Minor, which suggests that those regions were familiar to him.³ He also knows details of other natives of those parts, such as Aratus, the astronomer of Cilicia,⁴ and Apollonius of Tyana, about whom he adds further facts to those mentioned by his opponent.⁵ When he mentions the heroes of the Church, there is one about whom he gives details, namely, Polycarp of Smyrna, concerning whom he records stories like those given in the *Vita Polycarpi*, which may have formed a local tradition.⁶ It is true that he turns to the West for the rest of his list, which has led Duchesne to the surmise that the author had visited Rome. And he recalls traditions about both S. Peter and S. Paul at Rome, which might suggest that he was linked with that part of the world,⁷ were it not that he speaks elsewhere of the Romans as "a barbarian race."⁸ Whether all this accords with the authorship of such a small-minded man as the Macarius of the Oak, who accused another of the same tendency which is so plainly seen in the *Apocriticus*, is very doubtful.

It must be remembered that the title "Of Magnesia" does not necessarily imply that he was bishop there. It is often used of the locality whence a man derived his birth or upbringing, as is the case with Joannes Damascenus, or John of Damascus. It seems better to picture

¹ p. xv.   ² *Apocr.* iii. 40, p. 138, ll. 21, 22.
³ *Ibid.* iv. 15, and iii. 43, p. 151.
⁴ *Ibid.* iv. 17, p. 191, l. 17.
⁵ *Ibid.* iii. 8, p. 66, l. 19.   ⁶ *Ibid.* iii. 24.
⁷ *Ibid.* iv. 14, p. 182.
⁸ *Ibid.* ii. 17, p. 29, l. 12.

the author as a man bearing the very common name of Macarius,[1] who was not a bishop, but came from Magnesia, and, after perhaps having travelled as far as Rome, had settled in Syria at the time that he wrote his book. As he makes no attempt to connect his opponent with Syria, and only refers him to those regions in an entirely natural way, there is no reason for thinking that his language is merely part of a literary device. And a reason for the neglect of his work from the first may find an explanation in the fact that his theology was entirely different from that of the schools of Antioch or Edessa which were flourishing during the fourth century. His allegorical method of interpretation, which is even fuller of Origenism than that of Origen himself, would have been distasteful to the theologians of the neighbourhood, which would explain the fact that his book seems to have been unappreciated, and allowed to pass into oblivion, the only MS. of it to be found in the ninth century possibly owing its preservation to the portrait which formed the frontispiece.[2] Whether he wrote in the first decade of the fourth century, or at a later period, is impossible to decide with certainty. Harnack has evolved an elaborate theory of there being two men who are responsible for the heathen objections in the book, namely, Porphyry and an anonymous author who made excerpts from his book and issued them in the form of an attack on the New Testament and its teaching. Perhaps therefore I need not apologise for a similar attempt with regard to the answers, though in this case it is the earlier and not the later authority who is anonymous. I can imagine an Origenist writing a work, not far into the fourth century, in which he faced, probably by name, Hierocles and the arguments which he had brought against the Scriptures in his *Philalethes*,

---

[1] No less than twenty-four of that name are given in the *Dict. Christ. Biog.*

[2] His outlook is more Alexandrian than Antiochene, but had he belonged to Egypt, it is to that part of the world, and not to Syria, that he would have pointed for an example of the growth of monasticism.

a real dialogue being conceivably the foundation of his work. He was living in the East, but had visited Rome, and was also well acquainted with the eastern part of Asia Minor. He was a really great exponent of the Christian faith, and worthy to be ranked with some of the great fathers of that century. His work was seized upon by Macarius Magnes, the Bishop of Magnesia, who is heard of in A.D. 403, and worked into its present form, the original division of the two books of Hierocles being quite obscured. Nothing leads us to expect any great originality or literary talent or powers of Catholic exegesis from this Macarius. It well accords with what we know of him, that he should simply arrange another man's work. He carefully suppresses the names of both Hierocles and the man who had answered him, and alters just enough to make it appear a work of his own time, perhaps changing "200 years" into "300" (as Harnack suggested), and making the Trinitarian doctrine more definite [1] when opportunity offered. He does not trouble to change the locality from the East to Asia Minor, nor to add to the list of earlier heretics, but it is perhaps he who is responsible for the details about a local hero, Polycarp of Smyrna. As an opponent of Origenism, he would not have used such methods himself, but he allowed those he found to remain in their place. He may have curtailed the number of questions and answers to suit his purpose, which would explain the occasional failure of sequence in the questions, to which Harnack has called attention. It is surprising that so weighty a work was not carefully preserved by the Church. But if, in addition to the fact that it contained blasphemous objections to Holy Writ, it bore the name of an obscure bishop, of whom what was known was not particularly to his advantage, it can easily be understood how it was soon forgotten and was very nearly lost to posterity. The above theory of authorship is merely a suggestion; I leave it to others to improve on it.

[1] *Apocr.* iv. 25.

xxiv INTRODUCTION

THE TITLE OF THE WORK.

The double title is a strange one, "Monogenes or Answer-book to the Greeks (Μονογενής ἢ 'Αποκριτικὸς πρὸς "Ελληνας.)" Its very strangeness may have produced the further title found in the Athens MS., viz. "An account of the disputed questions and solutions in the New Testament" (περὶ τῶν ἀπορουμένων ἐν τῇ καινῇ Διαθήκῃ ζητημάτων καὶ λύσεων λόγος), with the added mention of five books. Neumann[1] long ago suggested that the title is to be transposed as "Monogenes or Apocriticus to the Greeks," and this is tacitly accepted by Bardenhewer.[2] But the further suggestion that the title *Monogenes*, as applied to God the Son, was probably made more use of in the first part of the work, now lost, is not borne out by the fact that of the seventeen times the word occurs in the extant books, fourteen are in six chapters of Book III. I prefer to think that the first part of the title was *Apocriticus*, as given in the MS., and I would offer the following explanation of *Monogenes to the Greeks*. If we consider the opponent's book to have been "Philalethes, to the Christians," it is natural that the answer should bear a name reminiscent of it. There is a certain amount of similarity between the word Philalethes (friend of truth) and Monogenes (Only-begotten), though the second is infinitely higher, and points to Him on whom reliance is placed for the answers. So we can understand the choice of such a title, with a further address "To the Greeks," to correspond to the dedication "To the Christians" in the earlier work. It may be added that there is a suitability in this dedication in each case. For Hierocles is said to have addressed his book "To the Christians, not against them,[3] and in the objections the second person plural is often used in addressing the hearers, as

[1] C. I. Neumann, *Jul. Imp. Lib. contra Christ. quae supersunt*, pp. 14-23, Lips. 1880.
[2] *Patrologie*, 1894, p. 550.
[3] Lactantius, *Div. Instit.* v. 2.

INTRODUCTION xxv

well as the singular, which is directed against a single opponent.[1]

THE LITERARY RELATIONS OF THE *APOCRITICUS*.

This part of the subject must be dealt with briefly. Let us begin with the Scriptures.

In the questions, quotations occur from Exodus, Deuteronomy, Joshua, the Psalms, and Isaiah, and also from the four Gospels, Acts, Romans, 1 and 2 Corinthians, Galatians, 1 Thessalonians, 1 Timothy, and the Apocalypse of Peter. With regard to the apocryphal book last mentioned, the fact that "its popularity seems to have been almost confined to the less-educated class of Christians,"[2] helps to explain how one came to know and quote it who only knew Christianity from outside.

In the answers, there are quoted, independently of the questions, Genesis, Exodus, Leviticus, Numbers, Deuteronomy, Joshua, 1 and 2 Kings, Job, the Psalms, Isaiah, Jeremiah, Daniel, and Habakkuk,[3] and also the four Gospels, Acts, Romans, 1 and 2 Corinthians, Ephesians, 1 Thessalonians, and 1 Timothy. Thus, in the New Testament, Ephesians is the only book quoted which had not been used in the questions. It is probable, but uncertain, that Macarius shows a knowledge of 2 Peter, but it is strange that, in answering the objection from the Apocalypse of Peter about the destruction of heaven and earth, he passes by the obvious parallel from 2 Peter iii. 12, and chooses that from Isaiah xxiv. 4. His attitude towards the Apocalypse of Peter is non-committal, but his substitution of similar passages from canonical Scriptures seems to suggest that it did not form part of his canon. With regard to the text used, the quotations on both sides seem to have been mostly made from memory. But

[1] e. g. *Apocr.* iv. 24, p. 204, l. 21.
[2] M. R. James, *Two Lectures on the Newly-discovered Fragments*, Camb. 1892.
[3] Of Apocryphal books, Macarius quotes Bel and the Dragon (Daniel xii. 34) in iv. 12, p. 174, and refers to 2 Esdras xiv. 21-25 in iii. 10.

xxvi INTRODUCTION

Hierocles uses the text of Codex Bezae in quoting Mark xv. 34 as "My God, my God, why hast thou reproached me?" and also in John xii. 31.[1] In the latter case Macarius follows him, but adds that there is another reading "Now shall the prince of this world be cast down" instead of "cast out" (κάτω for ἔξω). This is the reading of the Old Syriac and some of the Latin versions.[2] Passing from the Scriptures, we may note that Macarius makes several indirect references to Apocryphal literature and legendary stories. His statement that milk flowed from the wound at the martyrdom of S. Paul,[3] is also to be found in Pseudo-Abdias and Pseudo-Linus.[4] The latter was translated into Latin in the fourth century, so it may well have been previously known further East. The *Acts of Paul and Thecla* is referred to in ii. 7, p. 6, when, in speaking of the way the Gospel divides kinsfolk, Macarius gives as an instance the parting of Thecla from her mother Theocleia.

As he is so steeped in the spirit of Origen, we shall expect to find considerable indebtedness to the similar apologetic works in which Origen had answered the attacks on the faith made by the heathen philosopher Celsus. There are at least four objections to the Gospel which are identical in their respective opponents, but in each case the defence of Macarius is entirely different from that of Origen, and although the *Contra Celsum* must have been known to him, he does not seem to have used it in writing his *Apocriticus*.[5] But it is with the writers of the fourth century that most similarities have been found, and it is the suggestion of the indebtedness of the *Apocriticus* to its literature which has inclined so many to relegate the work to the following century. There is no doubt that its explanation of the Passion as

[1] See *J.T.S.* of July 1907, pp. 561–562.
[2] See Burkitt, *Evangelion da-Mepharreshe*, vol. i. p. 449.
[3] *Apocr.* iv. 15, pp. 126 and 127, n. 1.
[4] Duchesne, *op. cit.* p. 37. Also *D.C.B.*, art. "Linus."
[5] For a discussion of the question, I must refer to what I have written in *J.T.S.* of April 1907, pp. 408–409. He certainly does not follow Origen's resolve not to use allegorical explanations in answering a pagan (*Contra Cels.* ii. 37).

INTRODUCTION xxvii

a deception of the devil, wherein Christ surrounded the hook of His divinity with the bait of His humanity, is the same as that of Gregory of Nyssa, Rufinus, and Amphilochius, but it has already been stated that the idea dates from an earlier time, and so the fact of dependence must remain unproven.[1] In the case of the suggested similarity between the list of heresies in Macarius and one in Epiphanius, it does not look as if either borrowed from the other.[2]

THE TEXT AND MSS. OF THE *APOCRITICUS*.

We do not now know the whereabouts of a single MS. The Athens MS., which was at first generally considered to be identical with the Venice MS. which disappeared in the sixteenth century, was fortunately collated by Foucart and Blondel while in the National Library at Athens, before it passed into private possession by being left by the curator Apostolides to his widow. It is a paper MS. of the fifteenth century, and is described by Duchesne as badly written, with many gaps. Its accuracy can only be tested by comparing it with the fragments which are quoted by Nicephorus and Turrianus, and a few MSS. containing fragments. In every case, many mistakes and corruptions are revealed in the Athens MS.[3] And besides this, Blondel has had to alter obvious blunders on every page, or to note that they have been corrected by a later hand. Nor is the text always to be trusted in the form in which he has been content to leave it. In the translation which follows, I have suggested a few obvious emendations, but more remains to be done, and, as the MS. is necessary for the purpose, it is particularly unfortunate that its present whereabouts is so uncertain.

This side of the *Apocriticus* was discussed at length a few years ago by Schalkhausser, who confined himself to the textual problem, and did not touch the literary

[1] See p. 19, and *J.T.S.* of July 1907, pp. 550–551.
[2] *J.T.S.* of July 1907, pp. 548–549.
[3] See *J.T.S.* of July 1907, pp. 569–571.

one.[1] He carefully sets forth the quotations preserved in Turrianus from the Venice MS., to prove that it was not the Athens MS. which he had before him. After a very lengthy discussion of the problem, he adds a piece of evidence (p. 112) which, if it is to be relied on, is sufficient in itself to prove the point. It seems that the Athens MS., which only contains three out of the five books of the *Apocriticus* (and even they are mutilated at both ends), consists of one hundred and twenty-five leaves, but an ancient catalogue reveals the fact that the Venice MS., which was complete, contained only one hundred and four.

Schalkhausser also cites certain other MSS. which contain the famous chapter (iii. 23) on the Eucharist, which is the most familiar and oftenest-cited passage in the *Apocriticus*. At the end of it they add the story of the convincing of a doubting brother, which is plainly an interpolation. Linked by a colon or a hyphen to the final words of the chapter that "that which is eaten remains unconsumed," comes the abrupt commencement of a narrative. "A certain brother was in doubt concerning the things which were consecrated, saying that they were not the Body and Blood of the Lord, but types of these things." It proceeds to tell of the vision he had, while the deacon was reading the Gospel, of the heavenly Child slain and offered for food, of his inability to eat the flesh thus given, and of its being turned into bread as a concession to man's weakness. There seems no doubt whatever that the story is a mere insertion, of a later date than Macarius. Perhaps some one who reads this may recognise the source from which it comes. But the fact of there being such an interpolation adds point to my own suggestion with regard to the passage about the Trinity, where there is a sudden change of style, and the use of seemingly post-Nicene terms for "Person" and "Substance." If the Eucharistic chapter tempted some one to interpolate, the passage on Baptism

---

[1] Georg Schalkhausser, *Zu der Schriften des Makarios von Magnesia*, Leipzig, 1907, being No. 4 of vol. xxxi. in *Texte und Untersuchungen*, etc.

INTRODUCTION xxix

in the name of the Trinity may well have done the same.[1]

THE THEOLOGICAL AND APOLOGETIC VALUE OF THE *APOCRITICUS*.

We may set aside the charges of heresy brought against the work by Nicephorus, who was biassed by its use by his opponents. He specifies the particular dogma in it derived from Origen as being the non-eternity of punishment, and in iv. 16, p. 187, we find a second and better beginning postulated of "the whole nature and substance of created things." He speaks of Christ in one place as of Him "Who seemed to be subject to human affections" (iii. 8, p. 68), but other passages are entirely opposed to anything Docetic. In one passage (iii. 14) he speaks of His manhood as having become divine after the Passion, but if his language is heretical, he is following his master Origen. The Virgin-birth is regarded by his opponent as well as himself as an essential part of the faith (iv. 28). The power of Christ's atoning death is set forth in iii. 9 and 14, and His Resurrection and appearances are shown in ii. 19 to rest on the power, not of men, but of God. His Ascension and present ubiquity are discussed in iii. 14, His Godhead and His manhood being for ever indissoluble. Allusion has already been made to the very definite Trinitarian passage in iv. 25.

With regard to the Church and the Christian life, iv. 25 and iii. 23 are of the chief value. The water of Holy Baptism has the power to cleanse from the stain of evil, nor is it the fault of the Giver if this grace is abused. The Eucharist is the plainest explanation of Christ's words about eating His flesh and drinking His blood, and is far more than a mere type. Bread and wine are produced from the earth which He made, and so bread is already in a mystical sense His flesh. But the bread of the Eucharist is not ordinary bread, but is "tilled in the blessed land of Christ."

In spite of its present obscurity, I believe the

[1] See Introd., p. xviii.

Apocriticus to rank as one of the great apologies for the faith. Others deal with outlines, but Macarius is unique in his defence of details, and, except for his frequent use of allegory, his answers are mostly sound in the light of to-day. It is a great thing for a man to answer so many cunning objections without involving himself in inconsistency. He shows his readiness to meet his opponent on his own ground, and an absence of narrowness which ought to appeal to the modern reader. For instance, when the Mosaic books are discredited as written long after Moses, he accepts a later date without any weakening of their authenticity (iii. 10). In answering the charge of discrepancies in the Gospels, he replies that details of expression are not the criterion of the truth of a fact, and in such narratives as those of the Crucifixion, the varied accounts may be truthful, and yet reflect the suspense of the crisis, the very strangeness of which had unnerved all who were present.

One is tempted to multiply illustrations of the teaching and methods of Macarius, but it is better simply to refer to the pages which follow. There are some who will look in them chiefly for the pagan objections of his opponent, which have a special value of their own apart from the answers.

I have thought it best and handiest not to follow the plan of giving about seven questions in succession and proceeding to give the answers. This involves much turning of pages in order to read the corresponding answer after each of them. I have therefore placed each question and its answer together, irrespective of chapters in the book. The only drawback to this is that it makes the little exordium with which Macarius begins each fresh series, seem somewhat out of place.

Let me conclude by saying that my great hope in writing thus on Macarius Magnes is that many to whom his name has meant nothing will regard him with interest henceforth, and that those who know something of the *Apocriticus* will be induced to study it again for themselves, and possibly to help in the solution of those interesting problems which are still raised in connexion with it.

THE APOCRITICUS OF MACARIUS MAGNES

BOOK I

[Lost, with the exception of the following fragment of Chapter VI, which is preserved in the *Antirrhetica* of Nicephorus, *Spicil. Solesm.* i. p. 332.]

CONCERNING Berenice,[1] or the woman with the issue of blood. . . . Berenice, who once was mistress of a famous place, and honoured ruler of the great city of Edessa,[2] having been delivered from an unclean issue of blood and speedily healed from a painful affection, whom many physicians tormented at many times, but increased the affection to the worst of maladies with no betterment at all, He made to be celebrated and famous in story till the present day in Mesopotamia, or rather in all the world—so great was her experience[3]—for she was made whole by a touch of the saving hem of His garment.[4] For the woman, having had the record of the deed itself nobly represented in bronze,[5] gave it to her son, as something done recently, not long before. . . .

[1] Or Beronice, which is equivalent to Veronica. Her name is also recorded in the *Acta Pilati* (see ch. vii. in Tischendorf, *Evang. Apocryph.* p. 277).

[2] All the other records, viz. Eusebius, Sozomen, Philostorgius, and Joannes Malalas, say that the statue was at Paneas. Nor is this contradicted by Macarius.

[3] κατόρθωμα, one of the favourite words of Macarius, thus linking this fragment of Book I with the rest.

[4] σωτηρίου κρασπέδου, perhaps "The hem of the Saviour's garment."

[5] The statue is minutely described by Eusebius, *H.E.* vii. 18. Sozomen (*H. E.* v. 21) says that Julian took it down and put up his own instead, but the *Chronicle* of Malalas (ed. Dindorf, p. 329) says it was still in existence in a church at Paneas, in about A.D. 600.

BOOK II

[The Athens MS. does not begin till Chapter VII. The first set of objections in the Book is therefore lost. Chapters VII–XI contain answers to five objections. This looks as if Chapter I was in the nature of an introduction, unless there were six objections, and Macarius has combined two of them in one answer, as he does more than once in the later part of his work.]

CHAPTER VII. This is an answer to an objection based on the words of S. Matt. x. 34 ff.: "I came not to send peace on the earth, but a sword. I came to separate a man from his father," etc.

The first part of the answer is lacking, and the rest is lengthy and diffuse. The following is a summary of it:—

[To those who wish to receive the heavenly armour Christ speaks thus: "This warfare will mean putting away all earthly thoughts and giving up all human dear ones. After the victory a heavenly Father will take the place of the earthly one who has been renounced. This is the only way to conquer sin. The man who prefers earthly relationships will not survive the fray, and is not a soldier worthy of me."

Success in such a warfare may be plainly seen in the deaths of the martyrs. They were able to leave all those that were dear, and take up their cross and follow Christ. This is what is meant by the "sword," which cuts relations from each other, as it cut Thecla from Theocleia.[1] Daughters have taken this sword and cut themselves off from their mothers either by martyrdom or virgins' vows. Sons of great men have left their family customs to practise abstinence. Nor are those angered who are left behind. Go through the cities of

[1] For the well-known story, see the *Acts of Paul and Thecla*.

the East, and the province of Syria,[1] and test my words. Look at the royal city of Antioch,[2] and see what countless divisions there are. Some marry, others refuse; some are luxurious, others ascetic.[3] In a single house the "sword" of salvation cuts them apart, doing so without wound or pain, for it cuts not bodies but dispositions asunder.[4]

If the words bear an allegorical meaning,[5] the man divided from his father means the Apostles separated from the law. The daughter is the flesh, and the mother circumcision. The daughter-in-law is the Church, and the mother-in-law the synagogue. The sword that cuts is the grace of the Gospel.]

CHAPTER VIII. Answer to an objection based on the saying: "Who is my brother and sister?" and the words which Christ added, as He pointed to His disciples, "Behold my brethren and my mother" (Matt. xii. 48–49).

[These words were a reproof to those Jews who regarded Christ as merely a man, and not the Only Begotten.[6] So He asks, "Who is my brother, if I am the Only Begotten? Who is my mother, if I created all things? What man, acknowledging mother and brethren, ever

[1] It is remarkable that a writer apparently connected with Asia Minor should thus refer to Syria. For the suggestion that it is a reference to his opponent's connexion with it, see Introd. p. xv.

[2] With the reference to Antioch, compare the mention of Edessa, another city of Syria, in Bk. I, ch. vi.

[3] The contrast is expressed thus: ἄλλοι ταῖς ἑταίραις συνεῖναι σπουδάζουσιν, ἕτεροι ταῖς μονηρίαις θέλουσι συναυλίζεσθαι.

[4] This passage scarcely justifies the argument which has been drawn from it, that a development of monasticism is here implied, such as only took place in the latter part of the fourth century. For there is no actual mention of the developed coenobitic life.

[5] Macarius, as a faithful follower of Origen, frequently adds to his first explanation a mystical one of this kind. Indeed, when in difficulty for a plain answer, he resorts to it at once, *e.g.* in Bk. III, ch. xxv.

[6] Μονογενής, the alternative title of Macarius' book, appears here for the first time, and is used three times in the chapter. See Introd. p. xxiv.

did the miracles I have done? As no such man ever has done or will do them, why call me a mere man with brethren? The man born blind saw the Godhead with the eyes of his soul, but you are blind to the brightness of such power in your midst. So I say to you as to blind men, 'He that doeth the will of my Father (with which mine is identical) is my mother and brother,' for in so doing he both brings me forth as a mother does, having conceived me in doing the Father's will, and he also is brought forth along with me, not by coming into personal subsistence,[1] but by being made one in grace of will. For he that doeth the will of my Father bringeth me forth in the fellowship of the deed, and is brought forth with me. For he that believes that I am the Only Begotten of God in some sense begets me, not in subsistence but in faith, being mystically present with that which is begotten."

Note that Christ does not specify any of His Apostles by name, but simply says, "He that doeth the will of the Father."]

CHAPTER IX. Answer to an objection based on S. Mark x. 18 and S. Matt. xii. 35. Come now, let us also make clear the question of those two sayings: "None is good save God," and "The good man out of the good treasure of his heart bringeth forth that which is good."

See how plainly here also Jesus dissociates Himself from man when He says, "None is good save one, even God." And without doubt Christ is Himself God, even as John says, "And the Word was God." Also the Saviour Himself, revealing the essence of His own Godhead, says, "I and the Father are one"; which means that undoubtedly He who spoke the words was God. Why, then, if He be God, did He deny that He was God, by saying, "None is good save one, even God; why callest

---

[1] οὐκ ἐν ὑποστάσει οὐσίας γενόμενος. In the light of other passages in Macarius, there is a special interest in his use of these words. See Introd., p. xviii.

thou me good?" If your desire is to pay a genuine heed to the saying, the subject will become clear and easily grasped, though it be disputed and a matter of discussion among many. A certain young man of comely appearance pictured in the Saviour's presence a state of righteous action,[1] imagining that He, who for man's sake had become man, was like other men, possessed of no relationship besides that which is mortal. This young man played the impostor and desired to show himself off as often receiving much praise at the hands of many, besides thinking that the Lord was an ordinary man. So it was not as God but as man that he addressed Him when he came near and said, "Good master." Christ faces the man who has such an opinion of Him by saying, "Why dost thou call me good when thou thinkest me a mere man? Thou art mistaken, young man, in holding the theory that I am mortal and yet addressing me as good; for among men there is nothing inherently good, but in God alone. So according to thee at least I deny that I am good, since I am reckoned as a man. For if thou didst hold the belief that God is in me, and the unalloyed nature of the Godhead, thou wouldst have decided that I bear affinity to the nature of the Good, and wouldst have had no doubt.[2] But since thou didst secretly steal away the good that is absolute, and dost bear unreasoning witness to the good that is relative,[3] thou canst not reckon me as a partner of this thy reckless act of theft. For do not suppose that I myself have ever used the word 'good' without due thought. For even if I said 'The good man out of the good treasure bringeth forth that which is good,' I do not call the man good absolutely, but relatively, whenever he performs some good action through sharing in that which is good. Take an illustration. The fire is warm, and that which is brought near

[1] νεανίσκος τις εὐπροσώπῳ σχήματι τοῦ Σωτῆρος ἔμπροσθεν δικαιοπραγίας ἐζωγράφει πολίτευμα. Or does εὐπροσώπῳ σχήματι mean "in specious form"?
[2] Reading ἐνεδοίασας instead of ἐνεδοίασα.
[3] Literally, good by nature (φύσει) and good by position (θέσει).

the fire is also said to be warm.[1] But one is called warm absolutely and the other relatively. It is not that the identity of name steals away the truth and has a single way of expressing the matter. Rather is the difference of the nature of each wont to determine the identity of name. Thus if any one calls the Creator good, and also that which is created, he makes it plain that in the one case the goodness is in Himself, and in the other case it is derived from another. Hence a man is good,[2] not as having this possession from his own nature, but as having obtained this advantage from another. But God is good, not as having received or won this from another, but as a good which is absolute, and as such is neither changeable nor visible."

This then must be the distinction in your mind with regard to what is "good." It will prevent you from thinking that Christ stultified His own words by saying, "No one is good save one, even God." For the absolute good, the inherent good, the archetypal good, the invisible and unchangeable good,—this, He declares, is unique, and the Godhead underlies it. But the relative good, the good that is easily altered, that does not stand steadfast, but suffers change,—this He connects with man, and also with any created thing; as for example when He called a fish or an egg good, by saying, "Ye know how to give good gifts to your children."

CHAPTER X. Answer to an objection based on S. Matt. xvii. 15: "Have pity on my son, for he is lunatic," although it was not the effect of the moon, but of a demon.

[In answering this question, we will also consider the apparently uncalled-for rebuke which Christ adds to the multitude, in the words "O faithless generation, how long shall I be with you?"

The dragon or demon was cunning enough to attack

---

[1] The same illustration is used in iv. 26, of the relation of God to the gods of heathenism.
[2] Reading ἀγαθός instead of ἀγαθόν.

BOOK II. IX, X, XI

the boy at the changes of the moon, so that men might think that his sufferings were due to its influence. Thus by one act he accomplished two objects, for he both tortured the boy's body, and suggested blasphemy to the minds of those who saw it, for if they ascribed it to the moon's action, they would naturally blame Him who created the moon.

Christ perceives that they likewise have been affected by the demon, and so calls them a "faithless generation," because of their ideas about the moon. By expelling the demon, He shows them their error.

S. Matthew does not prove, by saying that "a lunatic boy" was brought to Christ, that he really was under the moon's influence. Like a good historian, he recorded things as he heard them, not as they actually were.]

CHAPTER XI. Answer to an objection based on S. John v. 31: How is it that Christ said, "If I bear witness to myself, my witness is not true," and yet He did bear witness to Himself, as He was accused of doing when He said, "I am the light of the world"? (John viii. 12, 13).

[Such witness is not true in man's case, but it is in God's. The Jews thought Christ was only man, but it would have been a sad thing for the world if He had accepted their judgment and sought man's witness for His divine acts.

So He speaks as man when He does not bear witness to Himself, but seeks it from God. But it is as God that He says He is the Light, the Truth, etc., disdaining witness from his inferiors. He therefore simply allows that if, in their erroneous judgment, He is merely man, His witness is not true. Thus He contradicts, not His own statement, but their opinion about Him.]

38 APOCRITICUS OF MACARIUS MAGNES

CHAPTER XII. Objection based on the discrepancy of the Gospels about the Crucifixion.

The Philosopher.

But he with bitterness, and with very grim look, bent forward and declared to us yet more savagely that the Evangelists were inventors and not historians of the events concerning Jesus. For each of them wrote an account of the Passion which was not harmonious but as contradictory as could be. For one records that, when he was crucified, a certain man filled a sponge with vinegar and brought it to him (Mark xv. 36). But another says in a different way, "When they had come to the place Golgotha, they gave him to drink wine mingled with gall, and when he had tasted it, he would not drink" (Matt. xxvii. 33). And a little further, "And about the ninth hour Jesus cried with a loud voice saying, Eloim, Eloim, lama sabachthani? That is, My God, my God, why hast thou forsaken me?" This is Matthew (*v.* 46). And another says, "Now there was set a vessel full of vinegar. Having therefore bound a vessel[1] full of the vinegar with a reed, they offered it to his mouth. When therefore he had taken the vinegar, Jesus said, It is finished, and having bowed his head, he gave up the ghost" (John xix. 29). But another says, "And he cried out with a loud voice and said, Father, into thy hands I will commend[2] my spirit." This happens to be Luke (Luke xxiii. 46). From this out-of-date and contradictory record, one can receive it as the statement of the suffering, not of one man, but of many. For if one says "Into thy hands I will commend my spirit," and another "It is finished," and another "My God, my God, why hast thou forsaken me?" and another "My God, my God, why didst thou reproach me?"[3] it is plain that this is a discordant invention, and either

---

[1] σκεῦος οὖν μεστὸν τοῦ ὄξους σὺν ὑσσώπῳ προσδήσαντες. In the Christian's answer the reading is similar but not identical.

[2] παραθήσομαι, as some MSS.

[3] ὠνείδισάς με; This is the reading of Codex Bezae.

BOOK II. xii, xvii

points to many who were crucified, or one who died hard[1] and did not give a clear view of his passion to those who were present. But if these men were not able to tell the manner of his death in a truthful way, and simply repeated it by rote, neither did they leave any clear record concerning the rest of the narrative.

CHAPTER XVII. Answer to the objection based on the discrepancy of the Evangelists.

The Christian.

Thus far and in such words did he declaim, setting forth with boasting the Hellenic view. But we were not overcome by the din of his words, nor did we fear for our life. Though we shrank from speaking the essential word as the result of acquaintance with it, we spoke as the divine grace gave us help. Speaking as follows, we gave a clear interpretation of the Evangelists as preserving one tenor of a single record, though with interchange of phraseology.

No one seeks the truth that is in the nature of the facts from syllables or letters, but starting from the fact he estimates the divergences of language. For instance, if some one simply speaks of the rational as "man," and another as "mortal," another as "endowed with speech," and yet another as "human being," he will mention many things in word, but there will be one thing that underlies them all. And whether any one says "mortal," or "human being," or "endowed with speech," he means nothing else but "man." Similarly in the case of the outer garment. Whether a man speaks of a "mantle" or a "cloak" or a "robe" or "woven garment," he does not mean many things, but some one thing with an interchange of names. Thus the Evangelists, writing in their eagerness of what was once done at the Crucifixion, spoke one in one way and one in another, but they did not mar the record. So then, if one said

[1] δυσθανατοῦντα. The point of the saying is not quite plain. It would be more in keeping with the sentence to read δὶς θανατοῦντα, *i.e.* "one who died twice."

"vinegar" and another said "wine," they made no mistake. And in the case of the sponge and the hyssop do not think it strange when you hear it said, "Having bound a vessel of vinegar to a hyssop they gave him to drink"; and again, "Having filled a sponge with vinegar they brought it to him." For the reed and the sponge and the hyssop seem to point in one direction in their origin, for each of them comes as a wild plant, and afterwards is cut down. Therefore when he had to say "reed," he said "hyssop" on account of the similar course of their growth and cutting. And most particularly do they observe the rule of the record, and do not write a single thing beyond what was spoken then amid the seething confusion of that deed of madness.

For His accusers were Jews, and His judges were Romans, both of them a barbarian race,[1] which does not lay claim to the language of freedom, and has not grasped the subtlety of Hellenic education. Moreover, everything was at that moment being driven about in confusion; the earth was trembling from beneath as though smitten by a blow, and the rocks were being rent and struck by the crash. Then suddenly there fell a darkness that could be felt, and the sun hid the rays that belong to it. No one was then in his sober senses, but was blinded by the confusion of the elements, while the innermost recesses were shaken of sky and earth and under the earth. . . .[2] Tell me, then, who was sound in mind amid such a state of things as this? Who was strong in soul? Who had not been stricken in mind? Whose understanding was not harassed? Who did not throw out his words as if he were in liquor? Who was not like a cheap-jack in the obscurity of his utterances? Who did not behold the things that were coming to pass as a deep and mighty vision of their dreams? No man, young or old, no woman, whether aged or virgin, no one of tender age, was possessed of steady reasoning, but all were senseless as though

---

[1] The Hellenic point of view is remarkable, which classes the Romans with the Jews as βάρβαρον ἔθνος.

[2] Reading ὑπογείων instead of ὑπεργείων.

heaven's thunder were sounding in their ears, and all did different things, losing their wits and not preserving the sequence of things, nor reason, nor habit. Wherefore those who wrote recorded their frenzy and the strange happening that then befell in word and deed, without seemliness, but without a word of falsehood.

Again, it is not allowable for a historian to write anything beyond the things done or said, even though the language be barbarian. And you yourself have Herodotus who was not a foreigner, but a clever writer of history, but he put sayings of a foreign kind in his history, even barbarous names of mountains and rivers, which would never have been mentioned at all, had he not discovered them from somewhere and written them down, with more careful regard for truth than for purity of style. It is therefore not surprising if the Evangelists seem to record some things that are strange. For it was not their care that what they said should have force, but their zeal was to preserve the truth of what was stated. And even if some woman or some man said something that was not consistent or was a solecism, all their desire was only to set this down. For they perceived that in this way the record would be above suspicion before the world, if the writing of the history was unaffected, and not at all elaborate. Those who wrote these things were not descended from men who were educated or skilled in letters. And even if they had been educated, it was not fitting to rob the history of its unlettered expressions, and to adorn the action with cleverness of language, but rather to preserve the character of what was said in the way that it was spoken.

CHAPTER XIII. Objection, based on S. John xix. 33-35 (the piercing with the spear).

It will be proved from another passage that the accounts of his death were all a matter of guess-work. For John writes : " But when they came to Jesus, when they saw that he was dead already, they brake not his legs ; but one of the soldiers with a spear pierced his side, and forthwith came there out blood and water." For only John has said this, and none of the others. Wherefore he is desirous of bearing witness to himself when he says: "And he that saw it hath borne witness, and his witness is true" (*v.* 35). This is haply, as it seems to me, the statement of a simpleton. For how is the witness true when its object has no existence? For a man witnesses to something real; but how can witness be spoken of concerning a thing which is not real?

CHAPTER XVIII. Answer to the objection based on S. John xix. 33–35.

Pray do not let that passage trouble you either, in that it is only John who says: "When they came to Jesus, they brake not his legs," while the others do not record it. For when he alone said it, he is not deserving of rejection. Rather is he naturally to be praised, because in his zeal he called this to mind.

And indeed through saying this he has spoken something else greater still, which also preserves the mystery of the dispensation, and introduces the word of marvel. For he says: "One of the soldiers with a spear pierced his side." This was in order that the opened side might grant an inlet to the cleansing, which had hitherto been closed,[1] so that when the blood and water flowed like a spring, those who dwelt in the country of the captivity might be delivered by the blood, and those who had the stripes of their sins might be washed in the water. This then has been done, not in a superfluous way, but of intention, with the divine forethought as it were underlying it. For since [? the flow of death came from His side][2] the cause of salvation must needs also flow from His side From His side did the blow spring, from His side flowed also the spring of life.[3] From His side came the disease and also the healing. From His side was the wandering

---

[1] τὴν ἀποκλεισθεῖσαν εἴσοδον τῶν περιβόλων λάβῃ τῆς κάθαρσεως.
[2] Blondel here suspects the omission of a whole line in the MS.
[3] There is a play on the words πληγή, a blow, and πηγή, a sprin

and from his side was the returning. From His side was
the pain, and from His side was the painlessness.

John, the one witness of this, which is itself the one
secret thing, testifies to that which is secret. John has
proclaimed that the smiting of His side has been made
good by His side.

This is true, even if he is the only one who says it,
and the other three do not. For another is telling the
truth when he tells of the beggar Lazarus and the rich
fool, though the other three do not mention them. This
is my answer so far.

CHAPTER XIV. Objection based on the Resurrection of
Christ and His manifestation of Himself (Matt.
xxviii. 6, etc.).

There is also another argument whereby this corrupt
opinion can be refuted. I mean the argument about
that Resurrection of His which is such common talk
everywhere, as to why Jesus, after His suffering and
rising again (according to your story), did not appear to
Pilate who punished Him and said He had done nothing
worthy of death, or to Herod King of the Jews, or to
the High-priest of the Jewish race, or to many men at
the same time and to such as were worthy of credit, and
more particularly among Romans both in the Senate and
among the people. The purpose would be that, by their
wonder at the things concerning Him, they might not
pass a vote of death against Him by common consent,
which implied the impiety of those who were obedient to
Him. But He appeared to Mary Magdalene, a coarse
woman who came from some wretched little village, and
had once been possessed by seven demons, and with her
another utterly obscure Mary, who was herself a peasant
woman, and a few other people who were not at all well
known. And that, although He said: "Henceforth shall
ye see the Son of man sitting on the right hand of power,
and coming with the clouds." For if He had shown
Himself to men of note, all would believe through them,
and no judge would punish them as fabricating monstrous

stories.[1] For surely it is neither pleasing to God nor to any sensible man that many should be subjected on His account to punishments of the gravest kind.

CHAPTER XIX. Answer to the objection based on the Resurrection of Christ and His manifestation of Himself (Matt. xxviii. 6, etc.).

Come now, and let us examine carefully that other action also which does not seem to you to have been rightly done. I mean why the Saviour, after having conquered the power of death and returned on the third day after His Passion from the depths of the earth, did not appear to Pilate. It was in order that those who have learnt how to do away with what is good, should not do away with the true fact. It was to prevent any base suspicion from base men from creeping in and stealing away the truth of the Lord's Passion. It was to prevent the unscrupulous from thinking that what took place was untrue, that the tongues of the Jews might not again hiss out the poison of the dragon, and that the fact might not become the universal scandal of the world.

For at once, if He had shown Himself to Pilate and the men of note who were about him, at once, I say, they would have spread abroad a statement, through the device of cheating, namely, that Pilate had nailed one man to the cross in place of another, through some plan of screening him; that he had done this as either himself deceived, or as being altogether put out of countenance with regard to Him, as is often wont to happen in such matters face to face.[2] Whence they would say that He had appeared to him after rising as the result of an intrigue, desiring to proclaim on authority the resurrection which had not taken place as if it had done

[1] These words seem to suggest a time of persecution as then present. See Introd., p. xvii.
[2] This is a literal translation of the puzzling words δυσωπηθεὶς λιπαρῶς πρὸς αὐτὸν ἅπερ φιλεῖ πολλάκις γίνεσθαι παρ' ὀφθαλμὸν τοιαῦτα.

BOOK II. XIX 45

so, and to strengthen by the Roman power a lying statement. Thus the matter was contrived as a mockery; the earnestness shown was mere play-acting. He who had had no passion was solemnly parading within the Prætorium as if He had had it and conquered it; some criminal had been delivered over to the cross in His stead; a trick had taken place in a court of law. He whom they had seized had got His freedom by a cunning device, and a form of jugglery; some other condemned man had been bound without exciting suspicion. And now Pilate, who had just judged Him according to appearance, had no more appearance of so doing, but was embracing Him who was still answerable, as if He were a friend. This action was a new one added to the evils already done against Judæa. Great is the resulting ridicule in the East. We Jews have an indelible shame in having fought against one man and not got the better of Him. See how much knavery the deceiver wrought, both while He lived and when He died in pretence.

[Macarius continues this lament of the Jews at some
length, picturing Pilate as telling the Emperor,
and orders being issued to believe what they
knew to be a fraud, while they themselves were
held up to odium for murdering the Saviour of
the race, and felt most acutely of all the extreme
publicity and officialism of the whole thing.]

Because of the likelihood of such happenings, and of such foolish talking on the part of the Jews, He did not appear to Pilate when He rose from the dead, lest that which had been done rightly should be judged as a trick of rascality and deceit. Nor did He approach men of repute of the company of the Romans, that there might not seem to be need of human support and co-operation for the confirmation of the story of the Resurrection. But He made Himself manifest to women who were not able to give help, nor to persuade any one about the Resurrection. Then He appeared to the disciples who were also themselves without power, and largely obscure because of their poverty. This He did fittingly and well, that the story of the Resurrection might not be heralded by the help of the power of the world's rulers, but that it might be strengthened and confirmed through men who were inferior and made no show in their life according to the flesh, so that the proclamation might not be a human thing, but a divine.

CHAPTER XV. Objection based on the words: "Now is the judgment of the world, now shall the ruler of this world be cast outside" (John xii. 31).

Any one will feel quite sure that the records are mere fairy tales, if he reads another piece of clap-trap that is written in the Gospel, where Christ says: "Now is the judgment of the world, now the ruler of this world shall be cast outside" (John xii. 31). For tell me, in the name of God, what is this judgment which then takes place, and who is the ruler of the world who is cast outside? If indeed you intend to say it is the Emperor, I answer that there is no sole ruler (for many rule the world[1]), nor was he cast down.[2] But if you mean some one who is abstract and incorporeal, he cannot be cast outside. For where should he be cast, to whom it fell to be the ruler of the world? If you are going to reply that there exists another world somewhere, into which the ruler will be cast, pray tell us this from a record which can convince us. But if there is not another (and it is impossible that two worlds should exist) where should the ruler be cast, if it be not in that world in which he happens to be already? And how is a man cast down in that world in which he is? Unless it is like the case of an earthenware vessel, which, if it and its contents are broken, a man causes to be cast outside, not into the void, but into another body of air or earth, or perhaps of something else. If then in like manner,

[1] This statement is one of the indications that these words were written when Diocletian had subdivided the Empire, and there was an Augustus and a Cæsar both of East and West.

[2] The argument varies strangely according as first one reading is taken, "cast outside" (ἔξω), and then the alternative, "cast down" (κάτω). Macarius in his answer at once notices the variation or reading, and argues, like his opponent, from both.

BOOK II. xv, xx

when the world is broken (which is impossible), he that is in it will be cast outside, what sort of place is there outside into which he will be cast? And what is there peculiar in that place in the way of quantity and quality, height and depth, length or breadth? For if it is possessed of these things, then it follows that it is a world. And what is the cause of the ruler of the world being cast out, as if he were a stranger to the world? If he be a stranger, how did he rule it? And how is he cast out? By his own will, or against it? Clearly against it. That is plain from the language, for that which is "cast out," is cast out unwillingly. But the wrong-doer is not he that endures force, but he that uses it.

All this obscure nonsense in the Gospels ought to be offered to silly women, not to men. For if we were prepared to investigate such points more closely, we should discover thousands of obscure stories which do not contain a single word worth finding.[1]

CHAPTER XX. Answer to the objection based on S. John xii. 31.

[Note that there are two readings: "cast out," and "cast down," and that the words which follow are: "I, if I be lifted up, will draw all men unto myself."

"World" does not mean all creation (which is subject to God), but *men*, who can subject themselves to some one else. And "ruler" does not mean the Creator, but an arch-demon that by guile rules man (who may be termed "the world within the world"[2]).

The verse means that Christ came to free them from his tyranny, casting him out and down from it. His rule was only recent, and not universal. He is said to rule "the world," although only "man" is meant, and there is more in the world than man.

For this identification of whole and part, we may compare the saying that a man is ill when one limb is so, or that all a cloak is poor because a tassel is lost. If

[1] lit. "a single windfall."
[2] Man is termed ὁ κόσμος τοῦ κόσμου.

it means everything that exists, we must remember that there are things invisible as well, thrones and powers, etc. Inspired language similarly uses whole for part, as when S. Paul says, "I am crucified to the world." He does not mean all the world, but the evil and fleshly part of it. If then S. Paul calls the fleshly side, which he painfully crucified, "the world," it was natural that the Saviour, when His cross was set up, should speak similarly of the weak and wavering human race.

Such was Christ's judgment in dividing men from their deceiver. Their former ruler was cast down, but they themselves were to be drawn upwards, as is suggested in *v.* 32. For He took a human body as the cord with which to judge His kin, and, binding it to His Godhead, He drew men up to heavenly abodes (for the race is bound to that body of His as by a rope, and drawn upward).

The "casting down" of the world's tyrant is not literal, but metaphorical. Supposing an earthly king passes judgment on one in authority, his fall is not from a hill or a housetop, but from his own power. He may still remain in the palace, but his authority is gone. So is it with the "strong man" whom Christ, as the "stronger man," cast down from his earthly power.]

CHAPTER XVI. Objection based on
S. John viii. 43, 44.

Come now, let us listen to that shadowy saying also which was directed against the Jews, when He said, "Ye cannot hear my word, because ye are of your father the devil (Slanderer), and ye wish to do the lusts of your father." Explain to us then who the Slanderer is, who is the father of the Jews. For those who do the lusts of their father, do so fittingly, as yielding to the desire of their father, and out of respect for him. And if the father is evil, the charge of evil must not be fastened on the children. Who then is that father, by doing whose lusts they did not hearken to Christ? For when the Jews said, "We have one father, even

BOOK II. XX, XVI, XXI 49

God," He sets aside this statement by saying, "Ye are of your father the Slanderer" (that is, Ye are of the Slanderer). Who then is that Slanderer, and where does he chance to be? And by slandering whom did he obtain this epithet? For he does not seem to have this name as an original one, but as the result of something that happened. (Whatever we learn, we shall understand as we ought.) For if it is from a slander that he is called Slanderer, among whom did he appear and work the forbidden action? Even in this, it is he who accepts the slander who will appear unscrupulous, while he that is slandered is most wronged. And it will be seen that it was not the Slanderer himself who did any wrong, but he who showed him the excuse for the slander. It is the man who places a stake on the road at night who is responsible, and not the man who walks along and stumbles over it. It is the man who fixed it there who receives the blame. Just so, it is he who places an occasion of slander in the way who does the greater wrong, not he who takes hold of it or he who receives it.

And tell me another thing. Is the Slanderer subject to human affections or not? If he is not, he would never have slandered. But if he is subject, he ought to meet with forgiveness; for no one who is troubled by bodily ailments is judged as a wrongdoer, but receives pity from all as being sorely tried.

CHAPTER XXI. *Answer to the objection based on S. John viii. 43, 44.*

[First observe that the verse following throws some light on these difficult words, namely, "He is a liar and so is his father"[1] (John viii. 44).

It is not that the Slanderer himself is the Jews' father. Nor does Christ say so. The words do not mean "You are of your father the Slanderer," but "Ye are of the

---

[1] This is the favourite patristic translation of the words Ψευστής ἐστι καὶ ὁ πατὴρ αὐτοῦ. (He is a liar and the father of it.) The whole argument turns on this questionable interpretation.

father of the Slanderer."[1] So the slander does not originate in himself, but in his father's promptings. In fact, their relation may be compared with that of the divine Son and Father. As those who believe the Son are brought to the Father as His heirs, so those who believe the Slanderer are dragged from their true Father by that Antichrist, and brought to his father who is the opposite of God.[2]

You want to know who the father of the Slanderer is, and what the slander was. You have heard of the fall of man from Paradise, and the slander of the serpent, when sin and death entered. It was thence that the Slanderer and his father got their terribleness. The serpent slandered men to God, and God to men. His "father" was a spiritual force who took possession of him. This was he of whom Job said, "He waxed headstrong against the Almighty" (Job xv. 25). This angel of deceit found the serpent, and by sowing in him the seed of slander, became the father of the Slanderer. When therefore the Jews rejected Christ's words and turned from His Father, they turned by their rebellion to the rebellious father of the serpent. That was why Christ spoke these words.]

Let this much suffice. If you approve, we will at this place solemnly conclude the argument, which has been sufficiently discussed. At some other time, if any point arises of the things that perplex, we will meet you again, and speak, as the divine gift grants us aid.

---

[1] ὑμεῖς ἐκ τοῦ πατρὸς τοῦ διαβόλου ἐστέ. This is another ambiguity, and Macarius makes it fit with his argument by a translation which cannot now be accepted.

[2] ἀντιθέος.

BOOK III

Proem (introducing the first seven questions by the Philosopher).

THIS is the third contest which our much-admired opponent prepared for us, after bringing a notable assembly of auditors. This, O Theosthenes,[1] we now unfold to your incomparable wisdom, relating to the best of our power the propositions which were the results of his reflection. When we had found a quiet spot, we spent a great deal of the day in discussion. He began to roll down upon us the loftiness of his Attic oratory,[2] so that the mighty throng of onlookers almost felt themselves joining in the contest, as they saw the terror of his wrath, which was meant to scare us away. Then, as though he were descending on us at a run from some hill, he threw us into consternation by troubling us with the force of his tongue. The beginning of his speech to us was as follows:—

Introduction to the answers of Macarius to the objections of Chapters I to VII.

When the exponent of Hellenic cunning had uttered these words against the divine teachings of Christ, he became silent for a space, as though there were no one to answer him. But we had the same feelings as the

[1] This is the friend to whom the book is dedicated. In the Proem to Book IV he is said to have helped to win the victory for Macarius by his support.

[2] The style of the questions is quite different from that of the answers. But whereas in the latter it is sometimes diffuse and somewhat turgid, the questions are in simpler and more direct language. The diction is, however, not without a strength of its own. Harnack says that this mixed style is modelled on Plato, Plutarch and Diodorus (*op. cit.* p. 97).

man who attacked with sword-thrusts a many-headed hydra, which, when one dragon-head was cut off, immediately produced many heads instead of the one. Feeling somewhat like this, we continued exhausted for a space. For no sooner did we with persuasiveness explain three or four or five propositions of his, than he, in imitation of the mythical hydra, when one was explained, put forward countless further questions, thus proposing endless study concerning the matters in dispute. He therefore forthwith, after raising questions on so many points, declared that it was for us to make answer to each. And we, recalling to mind the things he had spoken, replied as follows, beginning with his first inquiry.

CHAPTER I. How did Jesus allow Himself to be crucified with insult?

Why did not Christ utter anything worthy of one who was wise and divine, when brought either before the high-priest or before the governor? He might have given instruction to His judge and those who stood by and made them better men. But He endured to be smitten with a reed and spat on and crowned with thorns, unlike Apollonius,[1] who, after speaking boldly to the Emperor Domitian, disappeared from the royal court, and after not many hours was plainly seen in the city then called Dicæarchia, but now Puteoli. But even if Christ had to suffer according to God's commands, and was obliged to endure punishment, yet at least He should

[1] Apollonius of Tyana is said by Eusebius to have been the hero whom Hierocles set up in opposition to the claims of Christ. Born at the beginning of the Christian era, he became a philosopher of the Neo-Pythagorean School. He was an ascetic, and after travelling in the East and studying Oriental mysticism, he returned to Europe as a magician. He set up a school at Ephesus. His life, written by Philostratus, is full of fictitious stories. He was accused of treason by both Nero and Domitian, but is said to have escaped in each case by miraculous means. Further details of his escape from Domitian are given in the answer of Macarius in ch. viii. p. 66, l. 19. See p. 55. That his opponent regarded him as a hero is plain from Bk. iv. 25. (See p. 127.)

have endured His Passion with some boldness, and uttered words of force and wisdom to Pilate His judge, instead of being mocked like any gutter-snipe.

CHAPTER VIII. Answer to the objection based on the fact that Jesus allowed Himself to be crucified with insult.

Why did Christ, when brought before the high-priest and Pilate the governor, work no miraculous sign, and show no manifestation which seemed worthy of Him, nor any mighty word begotten of wisdom? Why did He appear in humble fashion, with utterance restrained and brief, and with heavy look?

It was in order that He might not make prophecies void of meaning, nor convict the sacred tablets of falsity, and make of none effect the toil of holy men, which they endured in their godly preaching of the message of the dispensation, as they wrote the mystery of His coming and unveiled the manner of His Passion long before. As the great Isaiah with voice of might says, "We have seen him, and he had no form nor comeliness, but his form was without honour" (Isa. liii. 2); and again, "a man smitten, and knowing how to bear sickness," and, "He was led as a sheep to the slaughter, and as a lamb he was dumb." And when speaking in the Person of Christ he says, "I gave my back to scourges, my cheeks to blows; my face was not turned away from the shame of spitting" (Isa. l. 6). And it is possible to find thousands of other things spoken by the holy prophets concerning Him. If then, as you suggest, He had uttered violent words when standing before the high-priest or the governor, He might indeed have smitten them with divine signs, and made these men afraid by some novel sight; He might have made them suddenly fall prone to the ground by some act of miracle; but He would have flung away all prophetic testimony, He would have disregarded the foreknowledge of the noble men of old, and stultified the words of those far-famed pillars; He would have made of none effect the divine revelations of the Holy Spirit, and He would simply have thrust aside all the expectation concerning Him, by fulfilling the dispensation of death by means of a phantom of the air, enslaving all things to the necessity of their fears, and constraining those who stood there by the force of His terrible brow.

And if by virtue of His Godhead He had made the rock tremble at His word, or shaken the house; if by a word He had produced a thick atmosphere or made an onslaught against the purpose of these savage brutes, then He would have done wrong by forcing the governor and the high-priests into subjection, He would have erred in compelling that which was evil[1] to admit of that which was just. And in this He would have come under the suspicion that He was working these marvellous novelties by means of magic. Accordingly, He would have been judged one of those who are regarded as Gorgons. If He had terrified Pilate with fateful portents, if He had frightened the priests with signs of a novel kind, if He had reduced the Jewish nation by the sight of apparitions, it would have resulted in that which was false combating the truth. For the wonderful works which had been done by Him would have admitted of a base suspicion among men, as though they had been wrought, not in accordance with judgment,[2] but merely in phantom form and lying semblance. Hence that which had come to pass in a godly way long before, whether on land or sea, whether in town or country, would have been maligned and judged as an illusive dream and not a reality. The other result would have been the non-fulfilment of the foreknowledge of the men of old time, for Jeremiah would have made a mistake in describing Him as a guileless lamb which was led as a sacrifice (Jer. xi. 19). But, in addition to this, there would have been no truth whatever in God being enrolled among men as the Word. For he who does things foreign to the nature of men does not remain among their number, but has a separate place of vantage of his own. Again, it would have been an utter lie when some

---

[1] Reading κακόν instead of καλόν. [2] κατὰ κρίσιν.

one else, speaking in the Person of the Only Begotten, says (Ps. lxviii. 22), "They gave me gall for food, and for my thirst they gave me vinegar to drink." For who would have dared, if struck by the lightning of His visitation, to make ready vinegar and offer Him gall? Who would not have trembled when they saw Him stern and fearsome, and combining with His words a terrifying look, first speaking and then forthwith concealing Himself, suddenly seen and then again invisible? Tell me, who would not have hidden himself from a countenance so full of portents? Who would have forged cross or tree, or goad or sharp nails? Who would have ventured to master Him who could not be mastered, or to seize as a man Him whose speech and deed were more than human? But if the cross had not been set up in the ground and no nail had been sharpened as a horn,[1] then the Passion would not have atoned through the Cross, nor would He have won healing by being pierced with evil. Nor would Habakkuk have made any clear revelation when he prophesied that He had horns in His hands, that is, the nails of the cross or its horn-like arms [2] (Hab. iii. 4). And again, Moses would not be worthy of credit in declaring Him first and foremost as life that was hanged (Deut. xxviii. 66). All would have been false, with no more than verbal truth, and far from the deeds of godliness, and so it would have been lawful to seek and expect another Jesus. For He who was heralded in the books of the Bible would not have come, for, as I have said, He would not have kept to such a fashion, but would have become man in the guise of a strange marvel. For if He had acted like Apollonius,[3] and had made a sport of His life by magic art, and, when speaking to the Emperor solemnly in the midst of his palace somewhere, He had been digging garden herbs at the same moment for those who kept gardens, the world would really have been justly deceived, and all creation would have been enveloped in the cloud of His deceit, since it would

---

[1] MS. κεφάλαιος. Some word like κεράταιος is what seems to be wanted.
[2] κεραίας.   [3] See note on iii. 1.

become the blind slave of a wizard philosopher, who was able by his knavery to snatch away his body and to conceal by his phantoms the name of godliness. If He had done this He would have been judged to be neither God nor the Son of God, but one of those wizards who spend their lives in cheating.

It was in order that no stumbling-block of this kind should turn His saving Passion into mockery, and that no suspicion of the laws of magic should tamper with the mystery of the dispensation, that He bore as man the experiences of insult. And yet no shame really touched Him, for He had the indwelling of One who was not subject to human affections,[1] and He did not admit the principle of shame. For just as a vessel when filled with fire within does not receive any impression of coldness that is brought to it from without, but thrusts it away by virtue of its inward warmth, so Jesus, having the indwelling of God, who is a divine Fire which cannot be destroyed nor spent, reckoned as nothing the coldness of the insults, and when He saw the revilings He was not influenced thereby. Just as a child, though he sees the laughter of his comrades being turned upon him in abundance, feels no shame, so Christ turned His face from the taunts of the Jews, as though they came not from men but from babes. Even as a rock which receives the trail of countless reptiles, feels neither trace nor track nor mark, for it carries moving things upon its natural hardness, and yet is not scratched by them at all; so Jesus, when the band of the Jews rushed upon Him like reptiles, remained firm and unharmed like a rock, receiving no shame by their impress.

And there is another reason for what He did. It was fitting that before the Passion He should have kept His divine power in check, in order that after it, and while it was in progress, and when He had burst the bands of Hades and cleft the earth and raised again a band of men with souls and bodies, and revealed the company of those who have passed from hence—He should show who He was that endured the Passion, and who it was that dwelt

[1] ἀπαθής. Cp. II. xvi. p. 27.

within Him. For if creation in one point[1] has been conquered by Him who seemed to be subject to human affections,[2] it was undoubtedly the God and Creator in Him that shook the world, and quenched the orgies of the foolish. And, indeed, it is not before the shock of battle but after it, that a soldier's qualities became manifest to his enemies. What greater thing could there be than to return from Hades after three days?[3]

We conclude therefore that Christ, by working no new marvel when brought before Pilate, illustrates a rule, and the conduct which results from it, seen in the theatre; namely, that a man should not rouse up the malice of the wild beasts against him by some novel and terrible mask, but should rather provoke them to the contest by a humble one, and should overcome their savagery by excelling both in skill and in strength. So He who had appeared humble in the contest, was seen to be most terrible after it, such as earth could not bear, nor could heaven endure to look upon the conflict, for the former fled hither and thither, and by its quakings made mighty efforts to escape, while the latter shut (so to speak) the eye of its light, and no longer had power to look upon that which was coming to pass. Concerning the Passion then, you may accept such points as these by way of answer.

CHAPTER II. Objection based on the saying: "If it be possible, let this cup pass from me" (Matt. xxvi. 36 seq., etc.).

Moreover, there is another saying which is full of obscurity and full of stupidity, which was spoken by

[1] ὑφ' ἕν.

[2] ὁ δοκῶν πεπονθέναι. This expresses one side of the Christological views then current, but not the side which recommended itself to later theology. See iii. 9 for a fuller treatment of the current theory of the Atonement which explained the humility of the Passion as a cheating of the devil, by concealing the real power of the Redeemer, and luring him to do his worst.

[3] The MS. gives τί γὰρ μεῖζον; κατελθεῖν κ.τ.λ. The use of this last word for returning from below is so unexpected that the correct emendation may perhaps be τί γὰρ μεῖζον; κατελθεῖν ἢ ἀπελθεῖν κ.τ.λ.

Jesus to His disciples. He said, "Fear not them that kill the body," and yet He Himself being in an agony and keeping watch in the expectation of terrible things, besought in prayer that His passion should pass from Him, and said to His intimate friends, "Watch and pray, that the temptation may not pass by you."[1] For these sayings are not worthy of God's Son, nor even of a wise man who despises death.

CHAPTER IX. Answer to the objection based on the saying: "If it be possible, let this cup pass from me" (Matt. xxvi. 36 seq., etc.).

(*This answer sounds strange and unsatisfactory to modern ears, but the latter part is given in full, for it raises the important question of its relation to the similar explanations of the Passion given in other Fathers of the period.*)

[Evidently it is Christ's inconsistency that is complained of. This is a saying where we must look below the surface, like doctors, who do not judge a herb by its being disagreeable, but look within it for some hidden use.

Christ's action in Gethsemane must be explained as follows: The devil had seen His mighty works, and was so convinced of His Godhead, that he was afraid to bring his forces against Him, and was slow in bringing on the predicted Passion. Had he altogether failed to do so, Christ's coming to take away sin would have been in vain, and the last state of the world would have been worse than the first. To prevent this misfortune, He lays bare His manhood, and *pretends* to be afraid of death, as a man might stir up a wild beast by making a noise.

---

[1] Reading ἵνα μὴ παρέλθῃ ὑμᾶς (MS. ἡμᾶς) ὁ πειρασμός. Possibly παρέλθῃ is to be translated "overcome you," but it looks as if the sentence had been confused with the παρελθεῖν in the previous one. Macarius in his answer only faces the general issue, and so does not mention this strangely incorrect quotation, which should of course have been ἵνα μὴ εἰσέλθητε εἰς πειρασμόν.

BOOK III. II, IX

Now man had met his fall through two things, a tree, and the food from that tree. In the case of the latter, Christ had already won back the victory by fasting from food; but it was only when He pretended to be hungry that the devil attacked Him as he had the first Adam, and was beaten. Just in the same way Christ now provokes him to a second conflict, by pretending to be afraid, so that by means of a tree He may counteract the deceit once caused through a tree, and when His tree is planted, He may slay from it him who himself shows his enmity in a tree.

So He really wants the cup to come quickly, not to pass away. Note that He calls it a "cup" and not "suffering"; and rightly so, as being associated with good cheer. And, indeed, He sipped nectar which was to bring life to the faithful. Thus was the devil to be finally ensnared, like a dragon with a hook.[1]]

This is what an experienced angler often does when he wishes to draw a weighty fish from the deep. By placing a small worm on the hook, he deceives him through the greediness of his belly and draws him up. Thus, when Christ wished to draw up by his throat the cunning and deceitful dragon who is hidden in the sea of life, and is the source of all mischief, He put the body like a worm round the hook of the Godhead, and, speaking through it, he deceived the metaphorical serpent of the spirit world. Wherefore speaking as man in a psalm of long before, He revealed this, saying, "I am a worm and no man" (Ps. xxi. 17). This worm, which was brought together with God the Word and then held fast in the sea of mortal life, provoked the mouth of the dragon against itself, and seized it at the moment that it seemed to be seized itself. This worm devoured in a hidden manner the tree of death; this worm creeping imperceptibly over the mount of impossibilities, aroused the voiceless bodies of the dead. This worm

---

[1] The same simile is found in Gregory of Nyssa, but it is not peculiar to him, for it is also in Rufinus and Amphilochius. See Introd., p. xix, for a discussion of the bearing of this on the date of Macarius.

by coiling round and encircling Hades strangled the commanders that watched over its garrisons, and seized the mighty ones there and bound them together. This worm, descending to the archives of the despotism, cut through the leaves with their record of sins, wherein had been written the transgressions of men, and destroyed them utterly. This worm made the devil's ark disappear, which he planned and made from the tree of transgression, wherein he had put away and hidden the robe of man's glory. This worm came into being without parentage and union; it is mystic, only begotten,[1] ineffable. Through this worm the mystic hook drew up the primeval[2] dragon, concerning whom one of the chosen holy ones prophesied, "Thou shalt draw a dragon with a hook."[3]

The points of our answer to you are sufficient, and the fact is quite plain that Christ deprecated His Passion for the sake of the dispensation of the world.

CHAPTER III. Objection based on the saying: "If ye believed Moses, ye would have believed me" (John v. 46, 47).

Again the following saying appears to be full of stupidity: "If ye believed Moses, ye would have believed me, for he wrote concerning me." He said it, but all the same nothing which Moses wrote has been preserved. For all his writings are said to have been burnt along with the temple. All that bears the name of Moses was written 1180 years afterwards, by Ezra and those of his time. And even if one were to concede that the writing is that of Moses, it cannot be shown that Christ was anywhere called God, or God the Word, or Creator. And pray who has spoken of Christ as crucified?

[1] μονογενής, the alternative title of the *Apocriticus*. In this same answer Christ has already been referred to as ὁ Μονογενὴς καὶ μόνος ἀγωνιστής.
[2] Or, Ogygian.
[3] Job xli. 1: "Canst thou draw out leviathan with a hook?"

BOOK III. III, X

CHAPTER X. Answer to the objection based on S. John v. 46, 47.

I must now answer you on a third point, as to why Christ said to the Jews, "If ye believed Moses, ye would have believed me, for he wrote concerning me." That Moses did write concerning Christ the whole world openly recognised, when he said a prophet should rise up in his stead, and spoke of Him as forming man along with the Father, and related His Passion in a mystical way in the bush, and wrote of His cross and revealed it by his rod, and of the golden pot (even His pure body which had the heavenly Word within as the food which cannot moulder), and thousands of things which are akin to these and follow from them.

But when you say that Moses' writings perished in the Captivity and were written again incorrectly by Ezra, you will find that they were written a second time with all accuracy. For it was not one who spoke to Ezra and another to Moses, but the same Spirit taught them both, and clearly revealed the same things to each of them. The Mosaic law was like a house that is pulled down by enemies, for the same Builder brought together each part and fitted them harmoniously together by the rule of His wisdom.

[So far from the Crucified not being called God in the Old Testament, prophecy is full of it. Look, for example, at such words as "The Lord's Christ" (Ps. xix. 7); "The Lord's Word shall go out from Jerusalem" (Isa. ii. 3); and "Therefore the Lord hath anointed thee" (Ps. xliv. 8).[1]

Christ spoke the words of the text in question, because, though Moses had written so much about Him, the Jews would not accept the fact.]

---

[1] It is curious that Macarius offers examples from the prophets and Psalms, but not from the law.

CHAPTER IV. Objection based on the incident of the swine and the demons (Matt. viii. 31, 32; Mark v. 1, etc.).

And if we would speak of this record likewise, it will appear to be really a piece of knavish nonsense, since Matthew says that two demons [1] from the tombs met with Christ, and then that in fear of Him they went into the swine, and many were killed. But Mark did not shrink from making up an enormous number of swine, for he puts it thus: "He said unto him, Go forth, thou unclean spirit, from the man. And he asked him, What is thy name? And he answered, Many.[2] And he besought him that he would not cast him out of the country. And there was there a herd of swine feeding. And the demons besought him that he would suffer them to depart into the swine. And when they had departed into the swine, they rushed down the steep into the sea, about two thousand, and were choked; and they that fed them fled!" (Mark v. 8, etc.). What a myth! What humbug! What flat mockery! A herd of two thousand swine ran into the sea, and were choked and perished!

And when one hears how the demons besought Him that they might not be sent into the abyss, and how Christ was prevailed on and did not do so, but sent them into the swine, will not one say: "Alas, what ignorance! Alas, what foolish knavery, that He should take account of murderous spirits, which were working much harm in the world, and that He should grant them what they wished." What the demons wished was to dance through life, and make the world a perpetual plaything. They wanted to stir up the sea, and fill the world's whole theatre with sorrow. They wanted to trouble the elements by their disturbance, and to crush the whole creation by their hurtfulness. So at all events it was not

[1] The Synoptic criticism is interesting, but he should of course have said "two demoniacs."
[2] Such passages are quoted freely, and not much stress can be made on the omission of the word "Legion."

right that, instead of casting[1] these originators of evil, who had treated mankind so ill, into that region of the abyss which they prayed to be delivered from, He should be softened by their entreaty and suffer them to work another calamity.

If the incident is really true, and not a fiction (as we explain it), Christ's saying convicts Him of much baseness, that He should drive the demons from one man, and send them into helpless swine; also that He should terrify with panic those who kept them, making them fly breathless and excited, and agitate the city with the disturbance which resulted. For was it not just to heal the harm not merely of one man or two or three or thirteen, but of everybody, especially as it was for this purpose that He was testified to have come into this life?[2] But to merely loose one man from bonds which were invisible, and to inflict similar bonds upon others; to free certain men happily from their fears, but to surround others with fears without reason—this should rightfully be called not right action but rascality.

And again, in taking account of enemies and allowing them to take up their abode in another place and dwell there, He is acting like a king who ruins the region that is subject to him. For the latter, being unable to drive the barbarians out of every country, sends them from one place to another to abide, delivering one country from the evil and handing another over to it. If therefore Christ in like manner, unable to drive the demon from His borders,[3] sent him into the herd of swine, he does indeed work something marvellous which can catch the ear, but it is also full of the suspicion of baseness. For when a right-thinking man hears this, he passes a judgment at once, forms his opinion on the narrative, and gives his vote in accordance with the matter. This

---

[1] There is no negative in the MS. A μὴ seems to be required, unless οὐ γὰρ is omitted before ἐχρῆν, as Harnack does. (*Op. cit.*, p. 36.)
[2] It seems best to read this sentence as a question.
[3] Blondel suggests τῆς ἐνορίου ἐλάσαι τὸν δαίμονα instead of MS. τὴν ἐνορίαν ἐλάσαι τοῦ δαίμονος.

is the way he will speak: "If he does not free from hurt everything beneath the sun, but pursues those that do the harm into different countries, and if he takes care of some, but has no heed of others, it is not safe to flee to this man and be saved. For he who is saved spoils the condition of him who is not, while he who is not saved becomes the accuser of him who is. Wherefore, according to my judgment, the record contained in this narrative is a fiction."

Once more, if you regard it as not fiction, but bearing some relation to truth, there is really plenty to laugh at for those who like to open their mouths. For come now, here is a point we must carefully inquire into: how was it that so large a herd of swine was being kept at that time in the land of Judæa, seeing that they were to the Jews from the beginning the most unclean and hated form of beast? And, again, how were all those swine choked, when it was a lake and not a deep sea? It may be left to babes to make a decision about all this.

CHAPTER XI. The answer to the objection based on the incident of the swine and the demons (Matt. viii. 31, 32; Mark v. 1, etc.).

So, now that this saying is made quite plain, let us examine the point at issue in another subject, namely the question of the man possessed with the demons, and the swine choked in the sea, and the swineherds who fled from the place.

Do not let it disturb you that Matthew speaks of two men possessed with demons, but Mark of only one. For Matthew speaks of two demons, but does not say that two men were possessed by them;[1] while Mark says there was one man, but many demons in him. For there must have been two chief demons, to which Matthew refers, of a specially evil kind, but other demons were assaulting the man along with them, or perhaps Matthew

---

[1] It is interesting to find that Macarius falls into the same mistake as his opponent, without seeming to discover it.

speaks of the number of persons[1] affected, when he says there were two men, but Mark indicates the nature[2] that suffered, without regarding the number. And indeed the common speech of educated men often follows this usage. For example, when the shepherd guards the flock, if a man speaks in reference to nature, he says: "The shepherd carefully preserves the beast." In saying this he does not refer to one beast, for they are many in number. But since, although the beasts happen to be many, they possess one physical nature, he says "beast" by virtue of that nature. But when he says, "The shepherd preserves the beasts," he speaks in virtue of their number. And there are other cases in which what is collective is wont to be spoken of singly. For instance, "The barbarian met the king," instead of "the barbarians," or "the barbarous tribe"; and "the king brought the soldier with him," instead of "the soldiers"; and one may find countless kindred expressions. So we must not be unduly worried, if one says there were two demoniacs and the other one. For, as I have said, the one showed the nature, indicating that it was human nature that was oppressed, while the other referred to the person, showing that there happened to be, not one of them, but two.[3]

We must now inquire how it was that the demons, though for a long time they had triumphed over reasoning creation with numberless torments, begged not to depart into the abyss, when their nature was searched by the ray of Christ's Divinity. We must also seek a reason for His yielding to their entreaty and suffering them to be sent into the swine as they demanded. I imagine that the demons, being terribly overcome[4] by the fire which shone from the sight of the Saviour, fevered as

[1] Macarius here uses the fourth-century word to express "person," viz. ὑπόστασις, keeping οὐσία for "nature." This passage naturally has some bearing on the one in which the words are given their technical use in speaking of the Trinity. See Introd. p. xviii.
[2] Viz. "human nature," as he explains further on.
[3] This explanation has been translated in full, not for its intrinsic value, but as indicating an interesting line of synoptic criticism.
[4] MS. χονευόμενοι. Blondel reads χωνευόμενοι.

they were by its warmth, strove to run to the waters and assuage the burning which oppressed them. And since, as having an incorporeal nature, they were unable to enter naked into the bathing-place of the waters, they looked to the herd of swine as a kind of ladder, so that they might enter it by their means and get rid of their burning heat.[1] And the demons, in their malice, do not seek the support of other beasts, but of those forbidden by the Mosaic law. They do this under the pretence of honouring the letter of the ordinance which was being ignored by those who inhabited Palestine at that time. But do not jump to the conclusion that the herd of swine belonged to the Jews. They were those of the Roman soldiers who had taken the cities of the East under the Emperor, for what the Romans call a "settlement."[2] For as the Jews were under treaty with the Romans, cohorts and companies of the Roman Power certainly dwelt in their provinces. For since the days of Augustus who caused all the world to be enrolled, and of Tiberius, and still earlier times, the Jews were Roman subjects, and all their country was tributary. Indeed, the Emperor simply appointed as king of Judæa Herod the son of Antipater, the latter being the man who supported the temple of Apollo at Askelon. He also sent out Pilate as governor and judge, who was himself a Greek, and the Romans had taken over all the offices among the Jews. For a long time the yoke of slavery hung round their necks, on account of their misdoings. Whence at that time there were herds of beasts belonging to Roman owners, and Roman managers answerable to their masters looked after their possessions. But all the same, the demons led the swine into the water, showing both their hostility and their guardianship of the law, and being inflamed accordingly.

As for Mark's record that Christ asked what the

---

[1] However far-fetched such a suggestion may sound, recent researches into the spirit world make it impossible to dogmatise on the impossibility of such happenings.

[2] σεδετον. MS. σεδεθρον, evidently formed from the Latin "sedeo."

demon's name was, as though He were ignorant of it, it was not in ignorance of the loathsome creature that He inquires what he is called, but in order that He might convict him from his own words, as a deserter from the heavenly kingdom. So He asks "What is thy name?" and he answers "Legion." He did not exist as such then, but he once was a legion, wielding the might of the kingdom above, even as it is written, "Can I not now pray to my Father, and he will give me twelve legions of angels?" (Matt. xxvi. 53). But that legion ran away, and was involved in the evil of desertion, finding the man a ready hiding-place; a sorry legion, indeed, which threw away its shield; not really a legion, but a bandit, stripping the earthly sphere and plundering it, and casting into incurable sorrows those who are taken captive. It was therefore in order that He might teach His hearers from what a ministry the legion had fallen, that He said "What is thy name?" His object was not to learn it Himself, for He knew, but that the bystanders might do so. For the demons, being greatly troubled, resorted to the former naming of their rank, in order that they might remind their great and kindly king, so to speak, of the goodwill of their former warfare, practically saying, "We were once a legion; we were the soldiers of thine impartial might. Remember that position which we once held, and have pity, and do not send us into the abyss. We were thy legion, but now are wicked bandits. Once we served, but now we plunder. Once we lived near thy palace; now we have come near to the parts beneath the earth. For then we dwelt in a pure abode; now we are befouled by mire and dirt. We claim to receive a worthy abode, in order that we may not be troublesome to those who belong to the Word. For as we have incurred the penalty of an evil smell, we seek that which may gladden us [1] as a vehicle for our evil smell. We entreat to depart into a herd of swine, since we have justly been cast out of the land of eternity. We do not yearn to seize herds of sheep or

[1] τὸ χαῖρον. This can scarcely be right. Probably the right reading is τὸν χοῖρον, *i.e.* "we seek the swine."

horses (for those beasts are clean and without pollution), but rather a throng of smelling and disorderly swine, in order that we may give a lesson to the inhabitants by what is done, and lay bare their own condition of foulness. For every one who is strong in mind and strong in thought, will be afraid to imitate a way of living which is foul and like the swine, perceiving that the demons drag such a one into the gulf of destruction. For from our evil case he will learn by some means or other of the rout we have suffered, and he will have no desire to obtain a like choice. Therefore, in order that we may be a living memorial, a great example, and a general warning, grant us the swine that they may guide us as strangers to the sea, in order that all may learn that we have not the power to control even small things, unless we are commanded and receive orders from the divine Spirit. The result will be that henceforth the whole world will look down on us, on the ground that we had not even authority over swine, and not even the herds in the country which were removed from it fell under our sway."

I think it was for the sake of wise action such as this that the Saviour did not send the demons into the abyss, but into a herd of swine, and through them into the sea. He was doing good in each thing, and giving right instruction, making manifest to men both the means of punishing the demons, and the warning not to desire the life of any unclean beasts. For if He had sent them into the abyss, as you suggest, it would not have been plain to them all, because it would not have been observed; it would have been left in doubt as not being perceptible, and a matter of suspicion as not being in bodily form. For any one might have suspected that they refused to obey Christ and did not depart into the abyss, but went to men who lived over the borders not far away, and wrought mischief that was worse still through running away. But as it took place, this was not so; but it became quite plain and obvious to all, through the destruction of the swine, that the demons left their human abode and went into the sea. Take this as a sufficient answer with regard to this story.

CHAPTER V. Objection based on the saying about the camel going through the eye of a needle (Matt. xix. 24, etc.).

Let us examine another saying even more baffling than these, when He says, "It is easier for a camel to go through a needle,[1] than for a rich man to enter into the kingdom of heaven."

If it be indeed the case that any one who is rich is not brought into the so-called kingdom of heaven though he have kept himself from the sins of life, such as murder, theft, adultery, cheating, impious oaths, body-snatching, and the wickedness of sacrilege, of what use is just dealing to righteous men, if they happen to be rich? And what harm is there for poor men in doing every unholy deed of baseness? For it is not virtue that takes a man up to heaven, but lack of possessions. For if his wealth shuts out the rich man from heaven, by way of contrast his poverty brings a poor man into it. And so it becomes lawful, when a man has learnt this lesson, to pay no regard to virtue, but without let or hindrance to cling to poverty alone, and the things that are most base. This follows from poverty being able to save the poor man, while riches shut out the rich man from the undefiled abode.

Wherefore it seems to me that these cannot be the words of Christ, if indeed He handed down the rule of truth, but of some poor men who wished, as a result of such vain talking, to deprive the rich of their substance. At any rate, no longer ago than yesterday, reading these words to women of noble birth, "Sell what thou hast, and give to the poor, and thou shalt have treasure in heaven," they persuaded them to distribute to poor men all the substance and possession which they had, and, themselves entering into a state of want, to gather by begging, turning from a position of freedom to unseemly asking, and from prosperity to a pitiable character, and in the end, being compelled to go to the houses of the

[1] He omits the word for "eye."

rich (which is the first thing, or rather the last thing, in disgrace and misfortune), and thus to lose their own belongings under the pretext of godliness, and to covet those of others under the force of want.

Accordingly, it seems to me that these are the words of some woman in distress.

CHAPTER XII. Answer to the objection based on the saying about the camel going through the eye of a needle (Matt. xix. 24, etc.).

[First study the narrative of the rich man coming with his depraved ideas. Christ wished to lead him up through his riches to what was higher.]

It was not the case, as you declare, that his riches shut him out from the kingdom; on the contrary, they would bring him in, if he were sober and managed them well. For as a soldier, when he uses his armour skilfully and well, becomes famous through it, and noble and conspicuous, and through it has an honoured entry to the king and makes a show within his palace; and again through it he becomes notable for an archer's powers, and has a peaceful time in the cities; but if he puts it on badly, and does not wear it as he ought, he becomes subject through it to capture by every foe, and through it he is cast out of the precincts as a traitor, and the spoil is taken off by the enemy; while through it he is seen to be unpurified, and so is set aside, and is punished by being cut off from life. And no one in all this blames the armour, but the man who did not use it rightly. No one, when he sees a man glittering in a suit of armour, says that it is this that causes his glory, but the zeal of him that uses the weapons.

[And it is just so with the man of letters, the statuary, etc.] And when a man has wealth and manages it well, he becomes a partaker of the heavenly kingdom, but when he abuses it, he is shut out from it, and does not suffer this experience as a result of the wealth, but as a reasonable result of his own baseness. Nor indeed is a man who improperly persists in his poverty praise-

BOOK III. xii 71

worthy on account of it. For many are poor, and they are not all praiseworthy, but each is properly so on account of his own experience. It is not his wealth that harms the rich man, but his unseemly course of life shows the wealth to be useless and unbeneficial; neither does his poverty lead the poor man up to heaven, but his bent of mind conduces to make his poverty profitable to his soul. For in rich and poor alike it is the nature of upright conduct and the disposition towards it that give lustre to his right action.

[Just as the same medicine will affect various people differently, so both riches and poverty may make a man either good or bad.] But in any case no one is put to shame in the life eternal who has lost his wealth through love of the kingdom of heaven, nor has he missed the mark through falling from his own possessions. For by giving what he has, he has received what he had not. By setting aside the earthly burdens which are grievous to be borne, he has received a fame which is light and unburdensome.

[Let me give you one instance out of many of the way that earthly riches may lead a man up to the heavenly. Job, as a rich man, fed the hungry and clothed the naked, and when the time came, he welcomed poverty aright, and looked on worms as goodly pearls. His riches always included virtue, and his poverty the love of his Maker.]

You must not therefore think that the Lord was making an absolute pronouncement when He said: "It is easier for a camel to go through a needle[1] than for a rich man to enter into the kingdom of heaven." For many are found within the kingdom who have become rich. And yet with good cause He casts[2] the rich man outside heaven, saying: "Hardly shall they that have

[1] Macarius follows his opponent in omitting the word "eye." But he does not follow him in using S. Mark's and S. Matthew's word for needle (ῥαφίς), but quotes S. Luke's (βελόνη).
[2] There is a gap in the MS., and a later hand suggests the insertion of "abundant wealth" (πλοῦτος ὁ πόλυς), which would therefore be the subject of the verb "casts."

riches enter into the kingdom of heaven." Those who have them and do not impart them, and give no share to those who have none, but confine their wealth to their sole and personal enjoyment of life, and never have friendly intercourse with poor men, neither giving comfort to pitiable poverty nor alleviating the wants of those who are in trouble; those who turn their converse away from them that deserve mercy, and avoid the griefs of the despised as if they were a pollution—these men are strangers to the kingdom of heaven.

No one comes within sight of a court of law without an advocate,[1] no one ascends the judgment-seat who bears the suspicion of an accusation, no one appears before a king who is implicated in any form of complaint;[2] no one departs to a feast who is soiled and stained, no one introduces feasting along with burdens, no one enters a palace who bears indications of a tyrant's instincts. It is as advocates of the rich that the poor exist; without them wealth is unprofitable in the sight of God. Marks of wickedness exist, and a man must cast these away and show himself free. Their existence betokens the suspicion of accusations, and the better way is to put this out of the way by one's own management, and openly serve the Divine. The accompaniments of abundance manifest themselves as spots and blemishes in men, and it is right thus to disperse these by better reasoning, and to press in to the blessed feast.[3] The guarding of possessions is a heavy burden, and it is righteous to shake off the burden and to march unencumbered to the assembly above.[4] Possessions turn into accusations of covetousness, and it is profitable to cast them away quickly, and to ride into the kingdom of heaven apart from them, if indeed a man truly believes

---

[1] These were called in by the parties in a suit to support their case, and gave their services without fee.

[2] The word is a technical one, connected with legal procedure.

[3] The word ἑστία signifies hearth or altar, but the allusion seems to be to the public table (κοινὴ ἑστία) at which ambassadors and others were entertained.

[4] The word used in Hebrews xii. 23.

BOOK III. XII, VI 73

that a kingdom of holy ones does exist in heaven. But if he does not believe it, why does he bother himself at all in arguing at random without faith?

CHAPTER VI. Objection based on the saying: "And in the fourth watch of the night he cometh to them walking on the sea" (Matt. xiv. 25; Mark vi. 48, etc.).

Come, let us unfold for you another saying from the Gospel which is absurdly written without any credibility, and has a still more absurd narrative attached to it. It was when Jesus, after sending on the disciples to cross the sea after a feast, Himself came upon them at the fourth[1] watch of the night when they were terribly troubled by the surging of the storm, for they were toiling all night against the force of the waves.

Now the fourth watch is the tenth hour of the night, after which three further hours are left. But those who relate the truth about that locality say that there is not a sea there, but a small lake coming from a river under the hill in the country of Galilee, beside the city of Tiberias; this is easy for small boats to sail across in not more than two hours, nor can it admit of either wave or storm. So Mark goes very wide of the truth when he very absurdly gives the fabulous record that, when nine hours of the night had passed, Jesus proceeded at the tenth, namely the fourth watch of the night, and found the disciples sailing on the pond. Then he calls it a sea, and not merely that, but a stormy sea, and a terribly angry one, causing them fear with the tossing of the waves. He does this in order that he may thereupon introduce Christ as working some mighty miracle in having caused a great and fearful storm to cease, and saved the disciples in their danger from the deep, and from the sea. From such childish records we know the Gospel to be a sort of cunningly woven curtain.[2] Wherefore we investigate each point the more carefully.

[1] The MS. reads δεκάτῃ, but this is plainly a confusion with the following sentence.
[2] σκηνὴν σεσοφισμένην.

CHAPTER XIII. Answer to the objection based on the saying: "And in the fourth watch of the night he cometh to them walking on the sea" (Matt. xiv. 25; Mark vi. 48, etc.).

[With regard to the "fourth watch," perhaps it is to be reckoned so as to mean the fourth "hour" of the night.[1] With regard to the use of the word "sea," note three things: First, the lake was certainly very like a sea if there were fishing-boats on it. Secondly, any gathering of waters may receive the generic name of "sea." Thirdly, apart from grammatical considerations, it is enough for us that the inspired author of Genesis tells us concerning the Creator Himself that "the gathering together of the waters He called seas."

The inner meaning of the incident must not be overlooked. Having just performed a miracle which showed His dominion over bread and the wilderness, Christ now proves to men by another miracle His dominion over water and the sea. The very elements join in the proof. The unwonted force of the storm reflects what nature feels at the fact that men should fail to recognise the creative Word. And the prophecy was thus fulfilled concerning Him who "walketh upon the sea as upon a foundation."

He prays to God, and then, after terrifying them through His Godhead, He pities them through His manhood. "It is I" brings them light after cloud, for He means "I who called you to be fishers of men, and fed the five thousand." Peter's faith wavers when he says, "*If* thou art such, bid me come to thee." When Christ says "Come," He means "Come to faith," for if Peter had actually been able to walk on the sea it would have falsified the above prophecy by making it apply to more people than one. Add to this his presumption and want of faith in saying "if," and his failure is explained. Christ saved him just as his tongue was making

---

[1] This would mean 10 p.m. instead of after 3 a.m. This is a somewhat unfortunate concession to the objector.

him sink (like a ship through its broken rudder), and taught him not to imitate the devil in the wilderness by saying "If thou art." So Christ says, "Come and learn. Thou needest this fourth watch even more than the ship. The darkness, the winds and the waves are all in thy lack of faith and thy presumption. The four constituents which should be blended in thy body are belied by thy doubting speech." Great, indeed, was the fall of this leading Apostle. Two shipwrecks were his—of the body and of the soul.

It was rightly "in the fourth watch" that Christ came to his help, for there were four elements that raged against them, namely, impenetrable atmosphere, rushing wind, moonless night, and roaring sea.

But there is a yet deeper allegory underlying the story. The sea denotes the brine and bitterness of existence; the night is human life; the boat is the world; those who sailed all night are the human race; the contrary wind is the devil's opposition; the fourth watch is the Saviour's coming. Note concerning this last point, that, as there are four watches in the literal night, so there are in human life. In the first watch the patriarchs helped life by their light; in the second, the law guided the boat of the world; in the third, the prophets contended for those human sailors; and in the fourth, Christ checked their fear and their foes, and ended the night by the light of His love for men. So when S. Paul says, "The night is far spent," etc., he refers to this dawn of the knowledge of God through Christianity.

Such an interpretation is supported by the passage about Elijah. His translation in a chariot of fire was foretold to him in the vision that he had in Horeb (1 Kings xix. 11), where the wind signifies the mighty word of the patriarchs, the earthquake is the Mosaic law, the fire is the prophets, and either the voice of thin air [1] is Gabriel's message, or perhaps the thin air is the body of Christ, and the voice is the Word speaking within it.]

[1] He here follows the Septuagint.

CHAPTER VII. Objection based on the sayings: "The poor ye have always, but me ye have not always" (Matt. xxvi. 11, etc.), and "I will be with you until the end of the world" (Matt. xxviii. 20).

Moreover, as we have found another inconsequent little utterance spoken by Christ to His disciples, we have decided not to remain silent about this either. It is where He says, "The poor ye have always, but me ye have not always." The reason for this statement is as follows: A certain woman brought an alabaster box of ointment and poured it on His head. And when they saw it, and complained of the unseasonableness of the action, He said, "Why do ye trouble the woman? She hath wrought a good work on me. The poor ye have always, but me ye have not always." For they raised no small murmuring, that the ointment was not rather sold for a great price, and given to the poor for expenditure on their hunger. Apparently as the result of this inopportune conversation, He uttered this nonsensical saying, declaring that He was not always with them, although elsewhere He confidently affirmed and said to them, "I shall be with you until the end of the world"[1] (Matt. xxviii. 20). But when He was disturbed about the ointment, He denied that He was always with them.

CHAPTER XIV. Answer to the objection based on the sayings: "Me ye have not always" (Matt. xxvi. 11, etc.), and "I will be with you always until the end of the world" (Matt. xxviii. 20).

[The difference may be explained by the fact that these statements were made at different times, and between them a change took place in the speaker Himself. It was before the Passion that He said they would not have Him always, seeing He was about to die. But after the Passion, He had overcome death and the laws of the body, and made man to be God.[2] So, speaking

[1] The quotation is abbreviated, and "always" is omitted. Macarius gives it correctly in his answer.
[2] ἅπαξαπλῶς τὸν ἄνθρωπον θεὸν ἐργασάμενος.

as God, He tells them His power is not circumscribed by time and space, but is present always and everywhere. After the Passion He passed through everything and sealed it as His own, heaven and earth and things under the earth.

This was true in the Passion also, as well as after it, as the following considerations will show:—

During the Passion itself, of course it was as God that He took the thief to His own Paradise, and thus showed that He was not circumscribed. How altogether vile are those[1] who twist His words into a mere promise for the future, by punctuating, "Verily I say unto thee to-day, thou shalt be with me in Paradise." For this is to circumscribe Him at the time of His death. But if it was He who rent the earth, darkened the sun, and brought up the dead, why could He not take the thief to Paradise?

Again, if the earthly sun shines everywhere, why not the Heavenly? So, when on the cross He was also everywhere, in Paradise, and in the Father. Even man passes the limits of space when he is in his dreams; can we suppose less of Christ when on the cross? Otherwise what were the use of the cross? The faithful got their requests and were healed during the ministry. Was there no guarantee to the faithful thief at the moment which was the very climax and sum of all Redemption?

The explanation of those scoundrels is quite untenable. They say He had power as God, but not yet as man, to take the thief to Paradise. Is such a distinction possible? Can you ask whether the faithful thief believed on Him as Divine or as only human? Such division is impossible, even in a man's faith. He is the same Lord, under many names; it matters not by which He is invoked, as Christ, or Jesus, or the Only begotten[2] of God; the effect of them all is identical.

---

[1] He compares them to Christomachi, for whom see Introd. p. xviii.

[2] Μονογενής, the alternative title of the *Apocriticus*, occurs four times in a few sentences.

Just as the smell of some herbal medicine would fill a whole house when placed in one part of it, so, as the healing medicine of Christ's body hung upon the cross, the odour of His Godhead spread through the whole house of the wide world.

Returning to the words of the objection, we conclude that after the Resurrection Jesus is circumscribed by nothing. In whatever part of the world the faithful may cry, He is there before they call Him. No separation of His Body is possible; it cannot be "unloosed," like the "latchet" the Baptist spoke of. Hence we assert that Christ both led the thief to Paradise, was present with the Apostles, and is not separated from the faithful until the end of the world.

But before the Passion, He could truthfully say, "Me ye have not always," because of the bodily separation which was about to come through His death.[1]

On the occasion when Christ spoke as above about the poor, the desire that the ointment should be for the poor, and not for the anointing of Him who for us became poor, originated with Judas, who valued the earthly ointment at three hundred pieces of silver, but in his madness sold the heavenly Ointment, which was emptied on the earth, at only thirty. But Judas must not occupy the stage; he must give way to matters more important. Pray produce another objection, as this argument is most useful to us.]

CHAPTER XV. Objection based on the saying: "Except ye eat the flesh of the Son of man and drink his blood, ye have no life in yourselves" (John vi. 54).

The Greek.[2]

But he, with a smile on his face, made reply in a fresh attack on us, saying: You are like the more

---

[1] Macarius speaks of His death as ὁ μυστικὸς θάνατος τῆς οἰκονομίας.

[2] The following paragraph introduces the next seven questions which are given in sequence.

BOOK III. xiv, xv

audacious among those who run in a race, and proclaim their victory until the contest comes, challenging many to run in the course; for you have taken up the same attitude, in your desire to bring in another inquiry from the starting-point, as one might say. Speak to us therefore, my friend, beginning from the following point :—

That saying of the Teacher is a far-famed one, which says, "Except ye eat my flesh and drink my blood, ye have no life in yourselves." Truly this saying is not merely beast-like and absurd, but is more absurd than any absurdity, and more beast-like than any fashion of a beast, that a man should taste human flesh, and drink· the blood of members of the same tribe and race, and that by doing this he should have eternal life. For, tell me, if you do this, what excess of savagery do you introduce into life? Rumour does not record—I do not say, this action, but even the mention of this strange and novel deed of impiety. The phantoms of the Furies never revealed this to those who lived in strange ways, nor would the Potidæans have accepted it unless they had been reduced by a savage hunger. Once the banquet of Thyestes became such, owing to a sister's grief, and the Thracian Tereus took his fill of such food unwillingly. Harpagus was deceived by Astyages when he feasted on the flesh of his dearest, and it was against their desire that all these underwent such a pollution. But no one living in a state of peace prepared such a table in his life; no one learnt from a teacher any knowledge so foul. If you look up Scythia in the records, and go through the Macrobian Ethiopians,[1] and if you career through the ocean girdle round about, you will find men who eat, live, and devour roots; you will hear of men who eat reptiles and feed on mice, but they refrain altogether from human flesh.

What then does this saying mean? [Even if there is a mystical meaning hidden in it, yet that does not pardon the outward significance, which places men lower than the beasts. Men have made up strange tales, but nothing so pernicious as this, with which to gull the simple.]

[1] See note on p. 125

Wherefore it seems to me that neither Mark nor Luke nor even Matthew recorded this, because they regarded the saying as not a comely one, but strange and discordant, and far removed from civilised life. Even you yourself could scarcely be pleased at reading it, and far less any man who has had the advantage of a liberal education.

CHAPTER XXIII. Answer to the objection based on the saying : " Except ye eat the flesh of the Son of man and drink his blood, ye have no life in yourselves " (John vi. 54).

The Christian.[1]

When the doctrine of godliness had thus been battered, and the foundation of the Christian bulwarks was almost shaken, we sought for the support of abundant arguments. Then we set up a fortified tower, so to speak, against the enemy, and trusting in this, we remained unwounded, although we had to face many wordy arrows, and we bore many an emptied quiver of cunning sophistry. And indeed when he who possessed his full armour at length began to grow weary from directing his bow against us with its sharpened darts and their rushing noise, we quietly directed our array against him and sharpened our weapons. We made our first letting-go, so to speak, by speaking to him and those with him about the flesh of Christ, showing that it was not strange or horrible when the Saviour said : " Except ye eat my flesh and drink my blood, ye have no life."

Consider, I pray you, and let us speak of the new-born child, and the babe that is brought forth on leaving its dark and humid abode. Except it eats the flesh and drinks the blood of its mother, it has no life, nor takes its place among men, but departs into the darkness of death. But if it receives a share of those natural springs and has abundant enjoyment of that kindred flesh, it is brought subsequently to full growth and becomes worthy

[1] The following paragraph introduces the answers to a sequence of seven questions. It should be noticed that the introduction shades off into the actual answer; cf. iv. 19.

of a better food and position, being enrolled among men, receiving its share of education and learning the marks of a noble citizenship. Later it sometimes takes its place among men who are great and famous, gaining experience as a general or an admiral or in many a council-chamber. And the reason of all these great blessings is the eating of the flesh and drinking of the blood of the mother who bore it.

[It is true that the nourishment comes in the form of milk, but milk is really the same as blood; it is only its proximity to the air that gives it its lighter colour. Even so frost will make water white, without changing its nature. Just as the Creator makes the foul waters of the abyss trickle out in a clear fountain, so do a woman's breasts, by an elaborate mechanism, gather blood from the veins, and send it forth in a palatable form.]

If then even boys tell us these things with persuasion as coming from physiologists, and learn the real truth about such matters (and you value these things highly as well as we), what is there that seems to you disturbing if the Gospel saying of Christ may be set beside them? For what was there horrible or strange in His teaching (as you seem to think), when He said: "Except ye eat my flesh and drink my blood, ye have no life in you"? For tell me, whereby is that nourished which is coming to the birth? Is it not by the blood of her that bears it, and the flesh, as has been demonstrated? This is through the cunning discovery of persuasive words, and yet it is by the same rule of truth. For if indeed Christ gave power to as many as received Him to become children of God, bringing them to their birth by some mystic word and then wrapping them in divine swaddling-clothes which cannot be described, pray tell me, whence will these children of God live and be nourished when they are just born? Will it not certainly be by tasting the mystic flesh and drinking the mystic blood of her that bore them? And it is none other than the wisdom of God that is constituted their mother, for she prepared her own table for her own children, and mingled her own wine for her own offspring, pouring forth richly from the two Testaments as it were from two breasts. It is indeed she who nourishes her recent offspring with her own flesh and blood, makes them comrades and renders them disciples of the heavenly kingdom, and then enrols them in the assembly of the Angels on high, bringing them into their pure council chamber, and, filling them with immortality and all blessedness, makes them like unto the Father, giving to them eternal life.

Now the flesh and blood of Christ, or of Wisdom (for Christ and Wisdom are the same), are the words of the Old and New Testaments spoken with allegorical meaning, which men must devour with care and digest by calling them to mind with the understanding, and win from them not temporal but eternal life. Thus did Jeremiah eat when he received the words from the hand of Wisdom, and by eating he had life; thus did Ezekiel feel sweetness when he ate the roll of the words (Ezek. iii. 3), and the bitterness of this present life was cast away. Thus did the saints one by one, once long ago, and again and again, by eating the flesh and drinking the blood of Wisdom, that is, by receiving in themselves the knowledge and revelation of her, live for aye with a life that will never cease. It was not only to the disciples that He gave His own flesh to eat and likewise His own blood to drink (for He would not have done right in thus offering the life eternal to some at a certain season, but not supplying it to others); but it was to all men alike in whom was holiness and the spirit of prophecy, that He gave allegorically this supply of food.

But at the end of the times He gave to the Apostles bread and a cup, and said, "This is my body and my blood." And in order that I may unfold the tale more clearly, and make plain the question of the passage, I will reveal to you the physiological side of eating (if indeed you are ready to put aside your preconceived views), for you may apprehend the mystery by that means. How then do we state the case? It is from the earth that we men have all come into being in our bodies, and it is by eating, in a certain sense, not the earth but its flesh, and drinking its blood, that we are prevented

from perishing. For the dry and wet products of the
earth are its flesh and blood. We live by eating and
drinking of these to our full satisfaction, but doing no
harm to the earth when we use up its flesh and blood.
For as we gladly gather the corn and the wine from it, we
enjoy ourselves by living on it. And now, for the rest,
lend me your ear with regard to the dispensation of the
mystery, and turn your understanding to the hearing of
it. How shall we express it then? In the beginning
the Only Begotten Son created the earth, and from the
earth He took man and wrought him, and from man
He took His body and became incarnate. If therefore
the body signifies the earth when simply stated,[1] and the
earth is Christ's creation through His operative word, as
being truly the result of His own making, and from this
earth were given in later time both corn and[2] wine and
also the body of man, and moreover it was this body
that Christ took upon Him, it was natural that when He
took the bread and the cup, He said, "This is my body
and my blood." It is no mere symbol of body nor
symbol of blood, as some have protested in the hardness
of their mind, but in very truth the body and blood of
Christ, since the body is from the earth, and the bread
and wine are from the earth likewise. How is it then
that no one else dared to say, "My flesh is food and my
blood is drink" (John vi. 55)? It is because no one
else has been made manifest as the maker and creator of
the earth, nor is it the individual creation and handiwork
of any one else, but it is the peculiar work of the Son of
God alone. It is for this reason that He likewise said,
"this is *Mine*, for the creation of the earth belongs to
Me and none other. For all men have come into being
by receiving their body from Me after the earth, but I,
before the earth was, wrought it, receiving it from no
one. And I became incarnate by taking a body from it,
or from what was My creation; for certainly it is from

[1] λόγῳ τῆς ἀρχαιότητος. This can mean "in the language of
simplicity," for it is difficult to see the reference to "the language of
antiquity." Is it "by His ancient word," as parallel to "His
creative word" in the clause that follows, viz. λόγῳ δημιουργίας?

[2] The MS omits the words for "corn and."

Myself that I offer you My bounty; for it is from the earth that the bread is ordained as a food for you, and the earth is of My manufacture. It is from the earth likewise that the body comes, and so it is My mingling. Therefore I give the bread and the cup, having sealed it as a result of the union wherein I the Holy One was linked with that which is earthly, declaring that this is my flesh and blood."

If it were Abraham, or any other righteous man, who had said, "My flesh is meat and my blood is drink," it would have been a great and impudent lie, for he would have been offering what was another's as if it were his own, and he would have been punished greatly for recklessly giving the bread and the cup to any and saying, "This is my body, and this is my blood." For it is not his, but belongs to the One who supplied it. Neither would the things eaten impart life to them who ate, as not having the living Word in combination with them. But the earthly body which is named the body of God led those who ate into life eternal, and Christ gave indeed His own body and blood to those who believe, by inserting the life-giving medicine of His Godhead. Therefore when He spoke of the flesh as bread and the blood as wine, He taught us plainly that the body is from the earth and the blood likewise, and that both possess the same essence.

But the common bread which is tilled on the earth, even though it be the flesh of the earth, has no promise that it contains eternal life, but it only grants those who eat it a temporary satisfaction, and soon vanishes, as being without share of divine spirit. But the bread that is tilled in the blessed land of Christ, being joined with the power of the Holy Spirit, at one taste gives a man immortality. For the mystic bread that hath inseparably acquired the Saviour's Name,[1] bestowed upon His body and His blood, joins him who eats it to the body of Christ, and makes him a member of the Saviour.

---

[1] κλῆσιν, which one would like to translate "invocation," but the phrase in the previous paragraph, "which is named the body of God" (θεοῦ σῶμα χρηματίσαν), suggests the translation given in the text.

BOOK III. XXIII, XVI

For just as the letter delta in the alphabet takes the force of the teacher and conveys it to him who is taught, and by its means leads him up to the teacher by putting him in touch with him, even so the body, that is to say, the bread, and the blood, which is the same as the wine, drawing the immortality of the immaculate Godhead, gives thereof to him that shares it, and by its means leads him up to the Creator's pure abode itself.

We conclude then that the Saviour's flesh is not wasted, neither is His blood used up by being drunk, but while he that eats it arrives at an increase of heavenly powers, that which is eaten is not exhausted, since it is akin to the nature which is inexhaustible, and cannot be divided from it.

Accept then, if you please, this mighty exposition of a mighty question.

CHAPTER XVI. Objection based on the saying: "If they shall drink any deadly thing, it shall not hurt them" (Mark xvi. 18).

Again, consider in detail that other passage, where He says, "Such signs shall follow them that believe: they shall lay hands upon sick folk, and they shall recover, and if they drink any deadly drug,[1] it shall in no wise hurt them." So the right thing would be for those selected for the priesthood, and particularly those who lay claim to the episcopate or presidency, to make use of this form of test. The deadly drug should be set before them in order that the man who received no harm from the drinking of it might be given precedence of the rest. And if they are not bold enough to accept this sort of test, they ought to confess that they do not believe in the things Jesus said. For if it is a peculiarity of the faith to overcome the evil of a poison and to remove the pain of a sick man, the believer who does not do these things either has not become a genuine

[1] He inserts the word φάρμακον into the text, which Macarius accepts without comment. The whole quotation is a loose one, and the clauses are in their wrong order.

believer, or else, though his belief is genuine, the thing that he believes in is not potent but feeble.

CHAPTER XXIV. Answer to the objection based on the saying: "If they shall drink any deadly thing, it shall not hurt them" (Mark xvi. 18).

[We must not take the words about the "sickness" and the "deadly drug" in too literal a sense. Otherwise we shall find them contradicted by two facts. First, those who are unbelievers may likewise recover from deadly drugs, so that the recovery need not consist in whether men are believers or not, but in the power of the drug. Secondly, many unbelievers run away at the first sign of sickness, but we must not therefore argue that those who stay to tend the sick are believers in consequence. Such literal and manward tests will not do, or we shall have people boasting of their faith simply because they have some skill in nursing.

So the "deadly drug" must be taken in a less literal sense, and this "death" is like that wherein S. Paul says, "We are buried with Him in baptism." Here there is a "deadly drug" which actually saves men from the tyranny of sin. For to drink this in faith means the death of the savage nature within, without any harm being received. So that which harms unbelievers does not harm the faithful. We may illustrate this by a stepping-stone, which may be either a help or a stumbling-block; or by the blessing on the world which came from the fall of the Jews (Romans x.); or by the Cross, which causes both light and darkness.

"Laying hands on the sick" must have a similar spiritual explanation. Their "hands" are their practical energies, and the "sick" are changes in the seasons, which are often sick through such things as storms, or want of rain.]

Certainly Polycarp[1] is an example of this, for while

[1] Macarius, as belonging to the East himself, only gives details of Polycarp in the list of fathers he mentions, as the others were of the Western Church. The facts here recorded are to be found in the *Vita Polycarpi*.

he exercised the office of bishop at Smyrna, the season of standing crops was greatly sick, when the heaven was not concealed by the smallest cloud, and poured down from the sky a burning heat, scorching to a great degree the vast tracts of land that lay beneath it; and it dried up the moisture of the foliage, and the trouble caused no little difficulty to men. Then that great man of God came, and when he saw the inhabitants thus afflicted, he in a sense laid his hands by means of prayer upon the burnt-up season, and suddenly made all things to be well. And later, when the land was drowned with unlimited rain, and the dwellers in it were in a pitiable state of distress, this same Polycarp stretched his hands to the air and dispelled the calamity, by healing that which was hateful to them. And indeed, before he became bishop, when he was managing a widow's house,[1] wheresoever he laid on his hands in faith, all things were well. And why should I stay to speak of the blessings conferred on men by Irenæus of Lugdunum, or Fabian of Rome, or Cyprian of Carthage? Passing them by, I will say something about men of to-day. How many, by stretching forth their hands in prayer to the heavenly Ruler, for the invisible diseases of suffering which press grievously upon the souls of men, have healed the afflicted invisibly in ways we know not? How many by the laying on of their hands have caused to be well those catechumens who were in their former fever of transgression or disease, raising them to the new blessing of health through the divine and mystical leaven?[2] For the responsibility that is laid upon the faithful is not so much zeal in driving away the sufferings of the body (for he knows[3] that these things train a man, rather than overthrow the govern-

---

[1] There is little doubt that this is the right reading, for it accords with what is related in the *Vita Polycarpi*. The MS. reading is not χήρας but χεῖρας, before which διὰ must be inserted if it is to be translated, *i. e.* "supporting his life by means of his hands."

[2] *i. e.* Baptism.

[3] The use of the singular suggests that the subject is "God" rather than "the faithful."

ment of his soul), as in driving away, by counsel and action profitable to the soul, those things which are wont to harm the understanding by enslaving the judgment of the reason.

Wherefore, as at least it seems to me, the answer on this point is such as to persuade those who hear it.

CHAPTER XVII. Objection based on the saying about faith removing mountains (Matt. xvii. 20).

Look at a similar saying, which is naturally suggested by it, "If ye have faith as a grain of mustard seed, verily I say unto you, ye shall say to this mountain, Be thou removed and be thou cast into the sea, and it shall not be impossible for you."[1]

It is obvious therefore that any one who is unable to remove a mountain in accordance with this bidding, is not worthy to be reckoned one of the family of the faithful. So you are plainly refuted, for not only are the rest of Christians not reckoned among the faithful, but not even are any of your bishops or priests worthy of this saying.

CHAPTER XXV. Answer to the objection based on the saying about faith removing mountains (Matt. xvii. 19).

[It is the custom of teachers only to enjoin on their pupils what they do themselves. But Christ never removed any mountain in Palestine, nor would there be any point in removing the hills He had founded for ever. Even if the believer had the power to do so, he would be prevented by the words of Scripture (Ps. xcii. 1), "He made fast the world, which shall not be shaken." So there must be some other meaning in the words.

---

[1] This is another case of a text apparently quoted from memory, which Macarius in his answer accepts as it stands, though he still further alters its last words. The truth is that two passages are combined. Ἄρθητι καὶ βλήθητι εἰς τὴν θάλασσαν is from Matt. xxi. 21, which is substituted for Μετάβηθι ἐντεῦθεν ἐκεῖ, καὶ μεταβήσεται of Matt. xix. 20.

The Apostles' faith was great enough to have the world put under their power, and so much greater was it than a mere mustard seed, that they could reduce cities thereby. They did not move literal mountains, such as Parnassus, or Ida, or Gargarus, or Taurus, or Bosphorus, or Sinai. But they rolled many metaphorical mountains away by driving away the *demons* which pressed upon men. To such mountains Jeremiah's words refer (Jer. li. 24), "I am against thee, O mountain, saith the Lord, which destroyest all the earth."

This explanation is confirmed by the context. Christ had just come down from the literal mountain and cast the demon from the boy who was called lunatic, and the words we are discussing were added when He told His disciples that it was because of their unbelief that they themselves had been unable to free the boy from the demon. So when He says "To *this* mountain," He means "That which has just been removed by Me from the afflicted boy." Had He simply said "a mountain" it might have meant a literal one, but as He said "this mountain," He showed that He was speaking of the demon, as being something which exalts itself against the knowledge of God.

Already He had cast many such mountains into the sea from their human habitations, when He drove those who were called legion along with the swine into the lake. In both places you must take the words as allegorical.]

CHAPTER XVIII. Objection based on the saying: "Cast thyself down" (Matt. iv. 6–7).

Come now, let us here mention another saying to you. Why is it that when the tempter tells Jesus "Cast thyself down from the temple,"[1] He does not do it, but says to him, "Thou shalt not tempt the Lord thy God," whereby it seems to me that He spoke in fear of the danger from the fall? For if, as you declare, He not only did various other miracles, but even raised up dead

[1] The addition to the text of "from the temple" is by way of explanation.

men by His word alone, He ought to have shown forthwith that He was capable of delivering others from danger by hurling Himself down from the height, and not receiving any bodily harm thereby. And the more so, because there is a passage of Scripture somewhere which says with regard to Him, "In their hands they shall bear thee up, lest thou dash thy foot against a stone." So the really fair thing to do, was to demonstrate to those who were present in the temple that He was God's Son, and was able to deliver from danger both Himself and those who were His.

CHAPTER XXVI. Answer to the objection based on the saying: "Cast thyself down" (Matt. iv. 6–7).

[Why did not Christ cast Himself down? Because it was the devil who told Him to, and thus to make peace with the adversary at the outset by taking his advice, is to give up the struggle. The advantage of casting Himself down was more than counterbalanced by this. Even to fulfil the words of prophecy, if it were at the immediate prompting of the devil, would be to act in concert and therefore in friendliness with him.

The question whether He should fulfil prophecy and obey the devil or not, is certainly a dilemma. But even if it were good in itself to do so, what follows makes it plain that it would have led to evil. For the devil was leading up to his final request, "Fall down and worship me." The other two requests were apparently harmless, but, had Christ yielded twice to his persuasion, it would have inclined Him to yield in the third case also. He sees the trick, and parries Belial's darts.

Certainly the prophecy referred to the Saviour, but it was a weapon which the devil had put in his own quiver, and therefore a piece of armour which Christ refused to use.]

CHAPTER XIX.[1] Objection based on Christ's saying to Peter: "Get thee behind me, Satan" (Matt. xvi. 23).

It is only natural that there is much that is unseemly in all this long-winded talk thus poured out. The words, one might say, provoke a battle of inconsistency against each other. How[2] would some man in the street be inclined to explain that Gospel saying, which Jesus addresses to Peter when He says, "Get thee behind me, Satan, thou art an offence unto me, for thou mindest not the things that be of God, but the things that be of men" (Matt. xvi. 23), and then in another place, "Thou art Peter, and upon this rock I will build my Church, and I will give to thee the keys of the kingdom of heaven"? For if He so condemned Peter as to call him Satan, and thought of him as cast behind Him, and an offence, and one who had received no thought of what was divine in his mind; and if He so rejected him as having committed mortal sin, that He was not prepared to have him in His sight any more, but thrust him behind Him into the throng of the outcast and vanished; how is it right to find this sentence of exclusion against the leader and chief of the disciples? At any rate, if any one who is in his sober senses ruminates over this, and then hears Christ say (as though He had forgotten the words He had uttered[3] against Peter), "Thou art Peter, and upon this rock I will build my Church," and "To thee I will give the keys of the kingdom of heaven,"— will he not laugh aloud till he nearly bursts his mouth? Will he not open it wide as he might from his seat[4] in the theatre? Will he not speak with a sneer and hiss loudly? Will he not cry aloud to those who are near

[1] A series of four attacks on S. Peter begins here.
[2] Reading Τί γάρ in place of the MS. εἰ γάρ. It may be noted that the next sentence begins with εἰ γάρ, and there may have been some confusion.
[3] As a matter of fact, the blessing upon Peter comes a few verses before the rebuke.
[4] Θυμέλη is properly the platform where the leader of the chorus stood, but here it is evidently a spectator's seat.

him? Either when He called Peter Satan He was drunk and overcome with wine, and He spoke as though in a fit; or else, when He gave this same disciple the keys of the kingdom of heaven, He was painting dreams, in the imagination of His sleep. For pray how was Peter able to support the foundation of the Church, seeing that thousands of times he was readily shaken from his judgment? What sort of firm reasoning can be detected in him, or where did he show any unshaken mental power, seeing that, though he heard what Jesus had said to him, he was terribly frightened because of a sorry maid-servant, and three times foreswore himself, although no great necessity was laid upon him? We conclude then that, if He was right in taking him up and calling him Satan, as having failed of the very essence of godliness, He was inconsistent, as though not knowing what He had done, in giving him the authority of leadership.

CHAPTER XX.[1] Objection based on Christ's words to S. Peter about forgiving "seventy times seven" (Matt. xviii. 22).

It is also plain that Peter is condemned of many falls, from the statement in that passage where Jesus said to him, "I say not unto thee until seven times, but until seventy times seven shalt thou forgive the sin of him that does wrong." But though he received this commandment and injunction, he cut off the ear of the high-priest's servant who had done no wrong, and did him harm although he had not sinned at all. For how did he sin, if he went at the command of his master to the attack which was then made on Christ?

---

[1] Contrary to his custom elsewhere, Macarius does not deal separately with this objection, but answers it along with the preceding one, by a very brief paragraph at the end of chapter xxvii. The fact that his opponent again alludes to the saying about "seventy times seven" in the next objection (chapter xxi.), may have made Macarius postpone mention of it until he dealt with that objection. But if so, he forgot it when the time came. It is one of the few instances in his book of his passing over one of his opponent's points.

CHAPTER XXVII. Answer to the objection based on Christ's saying to S. Peter: "Get thee behind me, Satan" (Matt. xvi. 23).

Now we must examine the objections about Peter. For truly they need testing and much explanation. Verily the foundation of the Apostles has been shaken by so great a clamour; the very apex of the gospel story has been obscured by such a cloud of unseemliness.[1] If Peter has been called by Christ an offence, and Satan, and a cause of stumbling; if Peter is convicted of having sinned in ways that cannot be forgiven, the whole band of the Apostles is attacked, and the roots of the faith are all but plucked up. It is right therefore to see the time and the place of this saying, in order that we may judge the matter and take hold of what it means.

[The blessing on Peter was an answer to his words at Cæsarea Philippi: "Thou art the Christ, the Son of the living God." Christ sees that he has not received this truth from "flesh and blood," nor even from angels, but as a direct revelation from the Father Himself.]

"Wherefore," he says, "receive a surname worthy of this grace, and be thou Peter (Rock-man),[2] showing to all the world a rock which is invincible and unshakeable, since the knowledge and the reasoning which thou possessest cannot be moved, in that thou hast borne witness this day to the fact that the blessed Essence cannot be shaken."

It was likely that the evil beast of deceit (the devil), hearing these words, and the witness which Peter gave to the Saviour, cunningly worked with all manner of zeal so as to strip Peter of his merit, and to overthrow the witness of Christ by the trickery of guile, and to alter the dispensation of the Passion. For he knew, he clearly

---

[1] Macarius echoes the word which his opponent had used at the beginning of his objection.

[2] In thus laying stress on the difference between πέτρος and πέτρα, Macarius supports the view that Peter is not here identified with the rock of the Church. It appears yet more plainly at the end of this chapter that the "rock" was the truth of Christ's divinity, on which the Church is founded.

knew that the Passion of Christ was a release from the tyranny of his wickedness, and so he was desirous of being a hindrance to the cross. So he prompts Peter to say: "Be it far from thee, Lord, this shall not be unto thee" (Matt. xvi. 22).

Christ recognises the real speaker, and addresses the devil and not Peter when He says: "Get thee behind me, Satan." Then He turns to Peter and rebukes him for obeying the prompting of Belial, with the words, "Thou art an offence unto me," etc. Peter's sudden fall from the highest to the lowest deserved such a rebuke, and at the same time it taught the disciples not to apply their petty talk to the eternal dispensation. What might have been the persuasion of the others, if they saw Christ on earth as Peter did, and then heard Peter persuading Him to postpone His glorious redemptive Passion and stay among the things of earth? His great faith had to have a great rebuke, and his great fall led to his great grief.

For note the height of his faith in the words, "Thou art the Christ," etc., wherein he was led up to the very court of heaven. He now knew the King upon His throne, and had it in his power to open his knowledge to those who came to him, but to keep it closed from those who were not fit for the beatific vision.[1] Hence he was said to have the keys of heaven, the power to open and shut it, and to lead men into it or out of it.

Note also the definiteness of Peter's words. He uses the article all through; it is not simply, "Thou art an anointed one, a son of a living God." For there are many anointed, many sons (the angels are called "sons of God"), many who are living, and "gods many and lords many." But the use of the article reveals the impregnable truth, and the unique nature of each. Speaking by the Holy Spirit, Peter thus reveals the impregnable rock, and gets his name of Peter (Rock-man) in consequence.[2] But

---

[1] Such is the sane and reasonable explanation which Macarius gives of this highly controversial question.

[2] See note on the earlier part of the chapter. The interpretation of the whole paragraph by Macarius is a valuable contribution to the literature of the subject.

BOOK III. xxvii, xxi 95

the devil tries to throw him from this rock on which he was so firmly set, by making him say what was unworthy of the promise, and express an unseemly sympathy. So Christ pierced him with a sharp rebuke.

Such was the rebuke implied in His healing the high-priest's servant,[1] whose ear Peter had cut off. Christ did not judge him by his stammering tongue, but by the inward desire of his soul.]

CHAPTER XXI.[2] Objection based on S. Peter's treatment of Ananias and Sapphira (Acts v. 1-11).

This Peter is convicted of doing wrong in other cases also. For in the case of a certain man called Ananias, and his wife Sapphira, because they did not deposit the whole price of their land, but kept back a little for their own necessary use, Peter put them to death, although they had done no wrong. For how did they do wrong, if they did not wish to make a present of all that was their own? But even if he did consider their act to be one of wrongdoing, he ought to have remembered the commands of Jesus, who had taught him to endure as many as four hundred and ninety sins against him; he would then at least have pardoned *one*, if indeed what had occurred could really in any sense be called a sin. And there is another thing which he ought to have borne in mind in dealing with others—namely, how he himself, by swearing that he did not know Jesus, had not only

[1] Thus briefly does he answer another objection of his opponent, as contained in chapter xx.
[2] It is at this point that the attack on S. Peter begins. Harnack (*op. cit.* p. 103 et seq.) considers that the opponent's work was here divided into two, a division which Macarius has quite obscured. He does not show why a book of excerpts from the fifteen books of Porphyry should have been thus divided, but he affords valuable though unintentional support to the theory that the work is the two books of the *Philalethes* of Hierocles. In this case this might well mark the beginning of the Second Book. As the beginning and end are lost, Harnack reconstructs the two parts as follows: the first part as containing $x + 10 + 13$ questions, and the second part $9 + 16 + x$ (p. 105 *n.* 1).

told a lie, but had foresworn himself, in contempt of the judgment and resurrection to come.

CHAPTER XXVIII. Answer to the objection based on S. Peter's treatment of Ananias and Sapphira (Acts v. 1–11).

[If you understand the circumstances, you will see that Ananias did wrong, and was punished for the general good.

The preaching of the Gospel and its wonders uplifted the first Christians to heaven, and men came from all directions to drink of the fountain of grace. They gave up individual possessions and joined all together, so that wealth ceased to exist in this spiritual society. Among others, Ananias and his wife offered their property to the common stock. When once given to Christ, it was no longer their own. It was therefore wrong to keep some back, though merely in itself such a deed does not appear so.

Peter at once cut out this evil, in order that the disease might not spread to the whole body of believers. The deed was not a wrong done to Peter, and therefore it did not receive his forgiveness;[1] but it was done to the Deity, and was an outrage on the faith. Besides, if no notice had been taken, they would have thought their hidden deed escaped Christ's notice, and so would have proceeded unrebuked to worse sins, and have infected others, like a pestilence, with the same ideas. To prevent this, Peter checks the disease, and drags up the weeds before they can spread over the field.

The above is proved by Peter's question: "Why did ye resolve[2] to tempt the Holy Spirit?" Then they were slain, by a blow, not (as you say) of a sword, but

---

[1] Thus briefly and in parenthesis does he answer what his opponent had said about the injunction of "seventy times seven." See note on the heading of chapter xx. This answer is excellent as far as it goes, but scarcely covers all the objection.

[2] The quotation, as often, seems to be from memory, as the reading is τί ὅτι ἔδοξεν ὑμῖν instead of συνεφωνήθη.

BOOK III. XXVIII, XXII 97

of the conscience, coming from the Holy Spirit of love. Peter is therefore without any blame for the death of either of them, which was sent as a warning to the rest.]

CHAPTER XXII. Objection based on the escape of S. Peter from prison (Acts xii. 5-11) and S. Paul's words about him (Gal. ii. 12 and 2 Cor. xi. 13).

This man who stood first in the band of the disciples, taught as he had been by God to despise death, but escaping when seized by Herod, became a cause of punishment to those who guarded him. For after he had escaped during the night, when day came there was a stir among the soldiers as to how Peter had got out. And Herod, when he had sought for him and failed to find him, examined the guards, and ordered them to be "led away," that is to say, put to death. So it is astonishing how Jesus gave the keys of heaven to Peter, if he were a man such as this; and how to one who was disturbed with such agitation and overcome by such experiences did He say "Feed my lambs"? For I suppose the sheep are the faithful who have advanced to the mystery of perfection, while the lambs stand for the throng of those who are still catechumens, fed so far on the gentle milk of teaching.[1] Nevertheless, Peter is recorded to have been crucified[2] after feeding the lambs not even for a few months,[3] although Jesus had said that the gates of Hades should not prevail against him.[4] Again, Paul condemned Peter when he said, "For before

[1] The opponent here shows considerable knowledge both of Christian methods of exegesis, and of the language of the Epistles.

[2] This is mentioned again in Bk. IV. ch. iv. when he says, "Peter, though he received authority to feed the lambs, was nailed to the cross and impaled." Macarius in his answer accepts the fact.

[3] This seems to have been a Christian tradition, as he states it unhesitatingly. Macarius tacitly refutes it by saying that the crucifixion was at Rome.

[4] It will be noticed that he puts a new and impossible sense in the words, necessitating the change of αὐτῆς (i. e. the church) into αὐτοῦ.

G

certain came from James, he ate with the Gentiles, but when they came he separated himself, fearing those of the circumcision; and many Jews joined with him in his hypocrisy"[1] (Gal. ii. 12). In this likewise there is abundant and important condemnation, that a man who had become interpreter of the divine mouth should live in hypocrisy, and behave himself with a view to pleasing men. Moreover, the same is true of his taking about a wife, for this is what Paul says: "Have we not power to take about a sister, a wife, as also the rest of the apostles, and Peter?" (1 Cor. ix. 5). And then[2] he adds (2 Cor. xi. 13), "For such are false apostles, deceitful workers." If then Peter is related to have been involved in so many base things, is it not enough to make one shudder to imagine that he holds the keys of heaven, and looses and binds, although he is fast bound, so to speak, in countless inconsistencies.

CHAPTER XXIX. Answer to the objection based on S. Peter's escape from prison (Acts xii. 5-11) and other inconsistencies.

[After killing James, in his hostility to Christ, Herod wanted to wreak public vengeance on Peter. It was not that Peter fled in fear; rather he was waiting to preach Christ in Rome and then welcome the glorious cross. It was not fit that Herod's malice should thus hinder the kindling of that Gospel torch which was to be lighted among the Gentiles.

As for the death of the soldiers, Peter was no more responsible for it than the stag would be, if the shepherd killed his dogs because it escaped from them. Herod did not owe his savagery to Peter, it was his own.

The object Peter continually had in view was to do

---

[1] This was a favourite subject of attack, and it will be remembered that the theory of a permanent cleavage between Peter and Paul has been built upon it.

[2] It is strangely unfair thus to imply that one passage follows after the other. The objector scarcely ever resorts to such subterfuges.

BOOK III. xxii, xxix, xxx 99

and say what was most profitable. It is this which must explain that conduct of which Paul speaks. His inconsistency was not for his own sake, but for the sake of saving both Jews and Gentiles alike. For the only way properly to influence the Jews was by showing reverence for the Mosaic law. Had he rejected it in favour of the Gospel, they would naturally have turned away from him. So he skilfully avoids the Gentiles' table while there is the chance of the Jews being scandalised, hoping in time to persuade the latter to walk according to the evangelic instead of the Mosaic rule. On the other hand, in order to attract the Gentiles, he ate with them when the Jews were not there. The result was profitable to both parties.[1]

When Paul speaks of " false apostles,"[2] he does not refer to Peter, but to those who were sent about the world by the Jews with encyclical letters.[3]]

The list of charges against Peter is a long one, but what I have said should suffice for you and those who sit with you. But if there lurks anywhere some other passage of the New Testament that is in dispute, announce it without delay.

CHAPTER XXX. Objection based on the inconsistency of S. Paul, in his circumcising of Timothy (Acts xvi. 3).

He remained a little while in deep and solemn thought, and then said: "You seem to me very much like inexperienced captains, who, while still afloat on the voyage that lies before them, look on themselves as afloat on another sea. Even thus are you seeking for other passages to be laid down by us, although you have

---

[1] In his anxiety to whitewash S. Peter from all charges, Macarius here may be said to overstate his case, for he fails to consider S. Paul's point of view.

[2] He misses the chance of scoring a point, for he might have pointed out the unfairness of the objection.

[3] The text adds the curious suggestion that they were consequently called στόλοι (expeditions) : οὓς ἐξαποστέλλοντες στόλους ἐκάλουν.

not completed the vital points in the questions which you still have on hand."[1]

If you are really filled with boldness about the questions, and the points of difficulty have become clear to you, tell us how it was that Paul said, "Being free, I made myself the slave of all, in order that I might gain all" (1 Cor. ix. 19), and how, although he called circumcision "concision,"[2] he himself circumcised a certain Timothy, as we are taught in the Acts of the Apostles (Acts xvi. 3). Oh, the downright stupidity of it all! It is such a stage as this that the scenes in the theatre portray, as a means of raising laughter. Such indeed is the exhibition which jugglers give.[3] For how could the man be free who is a slave of all? And how can the man gain all who apes all?[4] For if he is without law to those who are without law,[5] as he himself says, and he went with the Jews as a Jew and with others in like manner, truly he was the slave of manifold baseness, and a stranger to freedom and an alien from it; truly he is a servant and minister of other people's wrong doings, and a notable zealot for unseemly things, if he spends his time on each occasion in the baseness of those without law, and appropriates their doings to himself.

These things cannot be the teachings of a sound mind, nor the setting forth of reasoning that is free.

---

[1] Before the next sentence the MS. has "Ελλην in the margin, as a new heading, in order to mark the place where the actual objection begins. For the support thus claimed for the theory that Macarius is merely borrowing from a book, and himself turning it into a discussion, see Introd., p. xvii.

[2] Phil. iii. 2, *i.e.* a mere meaningless cutting.

[3] Gk. παραπάλλιον.

[4] The MS. gives καθηκεύων, which must be corrupt. The word, oddly enough, has just occurred in the previous answer of Macarius (ch. xxix. p. 122, l. 2, καίπερ καθηκεύων τοῖς Ἰουδαίοις πολλά. Foucart suggested πιθηκεύων in both places, as equivalent to πιθηκίζω (to play the ape), *Arist. Vesp.* 1290). But this requires the further emendation of πάντας to πᾶσι in the present instance. πάντας has just occurred in the same line, which may have caused the mistake.

[5] The speaker takes this in the moral sense, as meaning "lawless," as is clear from what follows.

BOOK III. xxx, xxxvii

But the words imply some one who is somewhat crippled in mind,[1] and weak in his reasoning. For if he lives with those who are without law, and also in his writings accepts the Jews' religion gladly, having a share in each, he is confused with each, mingling with the falls of those who are base, and subscribing himself as their companion. For he who draws such a line through circumcision as to remove those who wish to fulfil it, and then performs circumcision himself, stands as the weightiest of all accusers of himself when he says: "If I build again those things which I loosed, I establish myself as a transgressor."

CHAPTER XXXVII. Answer to the objection based on the inconsistency of S. Paul, in his circumcising of Timothy, etc.

When his chosen band had stirred up such a swarm of subjects against Paul, and the multitude of points[2] had at length grown quiet again like bees which have rushed to the attack in dense array, we, being as it were pierced all round by the stings of the difficulties raised, stood and fought against each in dire necessity, saying thus:—

[It is not right that you should abuse a great man for behaving towards those young in faith just as a teacher, or a doctor or a general does. For a teacher educates by imitating the stammering voice of his pupil, a doctor cures by placing himself in the patient's circumstances, and a general wins over a barbarian chief to his king by adopting his customs rather than by force of arms. Paul did similar good by being all things to all men. Sometimes he is the teacher, imitating Gentiles in order to educate them to the Gospel; sometimes the doctor, saying: "Who is weak, and I am not weak?" as if inflamed with the trouble[3] (2 Cor. xi. 29); sometimes

[1] The MS. ὑπόπυρος may be altered to ὑποπήρου.

[2] After all, he only deals with seven objections instead of eight at the previous bout, but only four of them were against S. Peter, and all the eight are here attacks on S. Paul.

[3] The words τῷ πόνῳ πυρούμενος are taken as part of the quotation in Blondel's edition, but there is no need to do this.

the general, softening men's prejudices by his strategy. So he went out to meet both those without law and the Jews, though he did not himself really feel as they.

Therefore he only adopted circumcision in order to enrich the law with the Gospel by giving way on one point. A good doctor may forbid a certain drug as being harmful, and yet in a bad case he may combine it with other drugs in order to overcome the disease. Just so, Paul rejected circumcision, and yet at a crisis he combined it with the doctrines of the Gospel.[1]]

CHAPTER XXXI. Objection based on S. Paul's inconsistency in claiming at different times to be a Jew (Acts xxii. 3) and a Roman (Acts xxii. 27).

This same Paul, who often when he speaks seems to forget his own words, tells the chief captain that he is not a Jew but a Roman, although he had previously said, "I am a Jew, born in Tarsus of Cilicia, and brought up [2] at the feet of Gamaliel, instructed according to the exact teaching of the law of my fathers." But he who said, "I am a Jew," and "I am a Roman," is neither thing, although he attaches himself to both. For he who plays the hypocrite and speaks of what he is not, lays the foundation of his deeds in guile, and by putting round him a mask of deceit, he cheats the clear issue and steals the truth, laying siege in different ways to the soul's understanding, and enslaving by the juggler's art those who are easily influenced. The man who welcomes in his life such a principle as this, differs not at all from an implacable and bitter foe, who enslaving by his hypocrisy the minds of those beyond his own borders, takes them all captive in inhuman fashion. So if Paul is in pretence at one time a Jew, at another a Roman, at one time without law, and at another a Greek,[3] and whenever he wishes is a stranger and an enemy to each

---

[1] It will be noticed that Macarius makes no attempt to argue from the special case of Timothy.
[2] He omits the words, "In this city."
[3] Surely this is a slip for "a Jew."

thing, by stealing into each, he has made each useless, robbing each of its scope by his flattery.

We conclude then that he is a liar, and manifestly brought up in an atmosphere of lying.[1] And it is beside the point for him to say: "I speak the truth in Christ, I lie not" (Rom. ix. 1). For the man who has just now conformed to the law, and to-day to the Gospel, is rightly regarded as knavish and hollow[2] both in private and in public life.

CHAPTER XXXVIII. Answer to the objection based on S. Paul's claim to be both a Jew and a Roman.

[Here again Paul showed the strategic powers of a general. If a general is driven out by his own countrymen, he no longer considers himself one of them, and overcomes them by joining some one else. Just so Paul was driven by the Jews into the hands of the Romans, and so he could say he was not a Jew but a Roman.

He was not wrong in calling himself a Roman, for by the Romé ($ῥώμη$ = might) of the Spirit he was to teach among the Roman nation.

Just as one of the Galatian race is called an Asian by living in Asia, so might Paul become a Roman, and yet remain a Jew. When he calls himself a Jew, he honours his countrymen; when he calls himself a Roman, he proclaims his nobility.[3]]

CHAPTER XXXII. Objection based on S. Paul's use of the law for his own advantage (as in 1 Cor. ix. 7, etc.).

That he dissembles the Gospel for the sake of vainglory, and the law for the sake of covetousness, is plain from his words, "Who ever goeth to war at his own charges? Who shepherdeth the flock and doth not eat of the milk

[1] Or, more literally, "a foster-brother of that which is false."
[2] lit. "Festering beneath the surface."
[3] Such is the strangely inadequate three-fold answer given to the objection. The play upon the word 'Ρώμη is quite characteristic of patristic interpretation. Macarius does not seem to have grasped that a Jew could be a Roman citizen.

of the flock?" (1 Cor. ix. 7). And, in his desire to get hold of these things, he calls in the law as a supporter of his covetousness, saying, "Or doth not the law say these things? For in the law of Moses it is written, Thou shalt not muzzle an ox that is treading out the corn" (*v.* 9). Then he adds a statement which is obscure and full of nonsense, by way of cutting off the divine forethought from the brute beasts, saying, "Doth God take care of the oxen, or doth he say it on our account? On our account it was written" (*v.* 10).[1] It seems to me that in saying this he is mocking the wisdom of the Creator, as if it contained no forethought for the things that had long ago been brought into being. For if God does not take care of oxen, pray, why is it written, "He hath subjected all things, sheep and oxen and beasts and birds and the fishes" (Ps. viii. 8–9)? If He takes account of fishes, much more of oxen which plough and labour. Wherefore I am amazed at such an impostor, who pays such solemn respect to the law because he is insatiable, for the sake of getting a sufficient contribution from those who are subject to him.

CHAPTER XXXIX. Answer to the objection based on S. Paul's use of the law for his own advantage (1 Cor. ix. 7, etc.).

[It is not in order to get something for himself that Paul introduces the comparison of the soldier and the shepherd, but in order to make the Corinthians thankful. For a soldier does his work faithfully only as long as the State pays him; and just so a herald of the Gospel will give his best work when his hearers respond to it. Similarly, the spiritual shepherd's encouragement is to see his sheep with fair fleeces and abundant milk. Again, the labourer sows the seed of the knowledge of

---

[1] The quotations are abbreviated. πάντως is omitted after δι' ἡμᾶς, and the middle clause of *v.* 7 is wanting. Macarius, however, makes use of the latter in his answer.

BOOK III. XXXII, XXXIX, XXXIII 105

God in his hearers' hearts, and is grieved if it does not bear fruit.[1]

Therefore it was in order to benefit his hearers that Paul introduced these things, and supported them with the witness of the law, so that they might show their gratitude. For the divine grace, though lacking nothing, demands a little answering tribute from those whom it enriches.[2]]

CHAPTER XXXIII. Objection based on his inconsistent attitude towards the law, condemning it in Gal. v. 3 and iii. 10, and approving it in Romans vii. 12 and 14.

Then he suddenly turns like a man who jumps up from sleep scared by a dream, with the cry, "I Paul bear witness that if any man do one thing of the law,[3] he is a debtor to do the whole law" (Gal. v. 3). This is instead of saying simply that it is not right to give heed to those things that are spoken by the law. This fine fellow, sound in mind and understanding, instructed in the accuracy of the law of his fathers, who had so often cleverly recalled Moses to mind, appears to be soaked with wine and drunkenness; for he makes an assertion which removes the ordinance of the law, saying to the Galatians, "Who bewitched you that ye should not obey the truth," that is, the Gospel? (Gal. iii. 1). Then, exaggerating, and making it horrible for a man to obey the law, he says, "As many as are under the law are under a curse" (Gal. iii. 10). The man who writes to the Romans "The law is spiritual" (vii. 14), and again, "The law is holy and the commandment holy and just," places under a curse those who obey that which is holy!

[1] The clause, "Who planteth a vine and doth not eat of the fruit thereof?" was omitted by his opponent from 1 Cor. ix. 7, but here Macarius plainly refers to it.

[2] No answer is here given to the difficulty about God not taking care of oxen, but there is a brief word of explanation at the end of the next answer (ch. xl. p. 107, ll. 12–17).

[3] This is quite different from the text of Galatians, "to every man that is circumcised." Perhaps the "one thing" comes from James ii. 10. Macarius accepts the quotation as it stands, and repeats it.

Then, completely confusing the nature of the question, he confounds the whole matter and makes it obscure, so that he who listens to him almost grows dizzy, and dashes against the two things as though in the darkness of the night, stumbling over the law, and knocking against the Gospel in confusion, owing to the ignorance of the man who leads him by the hand.

CHAPTER XL. Answer to the objection based on his inconsistent attitude towards the law.

[When he says that to do one thing in the law obliges a man to do all, he is not abusing the law, but pointing to its minuteness, and to that difficulty in carrying it out which Christ has freed us from, by coming to fulfil it Himself.

For a man who attempts to fulfil any part of it now may justly be accused of ignoring the complete fulfilment of it by the Only Begotten. He loses the effect of the Saviour's fulfilment, and yet cannot complete it himself, but is like one who has a hundred parasangs[1] to ride to reach a city, and only rides ninety-five; in which case he is no more in the city than when he started. If a man keeps countless commandments, and yet leaves one undone, it is as bad as leaving one gate of a city undefended out of thirty-five.

As an example of the difficulty in fulfilling the whole law, take two enactments, concerning the sabbath and circumcision. What is to be done with the babe born on a sabbath, upon the eighth day after its birth?[2] Here one rule contradicts the other. If two points are so hard, what of the whole? Indeed there are more rules than can be remembered concerning sacrifices, cleansings, etc. Such a burden proved too much for the Jews.

[1] This spontaneous introduction of a Persian measure of distance is a proof that the writer was near that part of the world. His subsequent suggestion of a city with so many gates indicates that there were large cities in his district.

[2] He chooses the example given by Christ Himself in John vii. 22-23, but can scarcely have that passage in mind, for it decides the difficulty.

BOOK III. XL, XXXIV

Only Christ could fulfil it, and so cancel it that none need be subject to it any more.

As a cubit-rule measures dimensions, but can itself only be measured by the man who made it, so the law, which is the measure of life, could only be measured by Christ, who made it, and finally sealed it up by placing the better measure of the Gospel beside it.

To try and fulfil what Christ has thus fulfilled, is to act in opposition to Him. Thus does Paul warn the Galatians. As for his calling the law "holy," etc., it was holy because the Holy One fulfilled it.

Again, when he brings in the witness of the law and quotes from it, "Thou shalt not muzzle the ox that treadeth out the corn,"[1] he is thinking of the apostolic band as the unmuzzled ox, which threshes that harvest which Christ has sowed. Hence he says, "Not concerning oxen were these things written, but concerning us" (1 Cor. ix. 10).]

CHAPTER XXXIV. Objection based on another inconsistency, in saying "The law entered that the offence might abound" (Rom. v. 20).

For see here, look at this clever fellow's record. After countless utterances which he took from the law in order to get support from it, he made void the judgment of his own words by saying, "For the law entered that the offence might abound"; and before these words,[2] "The goad[3] of death is sin, and the strength of sin is the law" (1 Cor. xv. 56). He practically sharpens his own tongue like a sword, and cuts the law to pieces without mercy limb by limb. And this is the man who in many ways inclines to obey the law, and says it is

[1] Macarius had ignored this part of the previous objection, and here his reference to the quotation can scarcely be called an answer to the difficulty raised, which seems to have proved too much for him.

[2] This is evidently a slip, as it is unlikely that he placed the Corinthian before the Roman Epistle.

[3] This correct translation must be given, rather than "sting," as Macarius develops the idea of a goad in his answer.

praiseworthy to live according to it. And by taking hold of this ignorant opinion, which he does as though by habit, he has overthrown his own judgments on all other occasions.

CHAPTER XLI. Answer to the objection based on S. Paul's saying that "The law entered that the offence may abound" (Rom. v. 20).

[There was naturally much wickedness in life, and this could not be corrected unless the law came to reveal it. Good and bad could not be distinguished till standards of right and wrong were set up. From such a life of ignorance and sin the law guided men to the life of light. But its enactments naturally revealed as sin what was not before understood as such, and in this sense it "made the offence to abound."

Sin was a "goad of death" to drive men from true life, and took its "strength" from the law, because the law punished sinners (see 1 Cor. xv. 56). A goad requires some one to wield it in order to make it deadly, and it was thus that the law wielded sin. Paul bids men flee from it, not to the law, but to Christ who is Master of the law. He does not destroy the law, but its work as "schoolmaster" ($\pi\alpha\iota\delta\alpha\gamma\omega\gamma\acute{o}\varsigma$) is done when it has brought men to Christ (Gal. iii. 23). The law is like the moon, and the prophets like the stars, which fade away at dawn before the Sun and His twelvefold crown of Apostles, and yet remain, though without power.[1]]

CHAPTER XXXV. Objection based on S. Paul's words about their not having "fellowship with demons" in 1 Cor. x. 20, and also what he says in 1 Cor. viii. 4 and 8 and x. 25–26.

When he speaks again of the eating of things sacrificed

[1] The above summary is in a very abbreviated form, but it will be seen that, unlike some of his defence of S. Paul, his line of argument is excellent, and is a sound interpretation of S. Paul's own attitude towards the law.

BOOK III. XLI, XXXV, XLII

to idols, he simply teaches that these matters are indifferent, telling them not to be inquisitive nor to ask questions, but to eat things even though they be sacrificed to idols, provided only that no one speaks to them in warning. Wherein he is represented as saying, "The things which they sacrifice, they sacrifice to demons, but I would not that you should have fellowship with demons" (1 Cor. x. 20).[1]

Thus he speaks and writes: and again he writes with indifference about such eating, "We know that an idol is nothing in the world, and that there is none other God but one" (1 Cor. viii. 4), and a little after this, "Meat will not commend us to God, neither, if we eat, are we the better, neither, if we eat not, are we the worse" (v. 8). Then, after all this prating of quackery, he ruminated, like a man lying in bed, and said, "Eat all that is sold in the shambles, asking no questions for conscience' sake, for the earth is the Lord's and the fulness thereof" (1 Cor. x. 25-26). Oh, what a stage farce, got from no one! Oh, the monstrous inconsistency of his utterance! A saying which destroys itself with its own sword! Oh, novel kind of archery, which turns against him who drew the bow, and strikes him!

CHAPTER XLII.[2] Answer to the objection based on S. Paul's words about having fellowship with demons (1 Cor. x. 20), etc.

Now that we have laid bare the full meaning of this passage, we will deal with the rest, if agreeable to you—namely, how it was that Paul forbade them to eat things offered to idols,[3] but he does not forbid them to take what was sold in the shambles, although it was well

[1] The verse is quoted in an abbreviated form.
[2] The full translation of this answer is given, as its language is curious and interesting.
[3] The answer at once makes obvious what the objection failed to state explicitly—namely, that S. Paul's inconsistency lies in his contradiction of the decision in Acts xv. that the Gentile converts were not to eat things offered to idols.

known that it was Greeks who did most of the slaughtering at that time.[1] So you may perceive in this the accuracy and wisdom of Paul, how he protects their daily life and forbids the godly to touch things sacrificed to demons, but he permitted his friends to eat what was sold in the shambles without asking questions. For the sacrifice of animals was at that time manifold, and different in various parts of the world. There was one kind to the spirits of the air, another to those on the earth, while there were other sacrifices again to those under the earth. For error, taking the deceitful serpent as its minister, whistled many a strain, charming and subduing with its deadly spells[2] earth, sea, air, and the things beneath the earth. So invisible spirits which flew in the air, which Isaiah sang of as flying serpents (Isa. xxvii. 1), demanded white and transparent sacrifices of birds, seeing that the air chances to be bright, and filled with light for the manifestation of the things that are below. But there are certain of the demons of the earth, which demanded herds of beasts for sacrifices which were black-skinned and dusky, seeing that the earth is by nature black and gloomy; and they ordered their sacrifices to be slain on lofty altars. Other demons of the regions beneath them enjoined that black offerings should be sacrificed to them in trenches, and that they should be buried alongside the remains of the things that had been slaughtered.[3] Other deceitful phantoms of things in the seas demanded sacrifices of black things that were winged and living, and ordered them to be sent down into the sea, since the sea is black and in constant motion. Seeing then that wickedness thus destroys the things without reason through those that possess it, by feeding in this pitiable way on a multitude of beasts and birds, the Apostle naturally forbade the faithful to touch such things.

You can verify these things from the book " Concerning

[1] This is an attempt to render καίπερ Ἑλλήνων ὡς ἐπὶ τὸ πλεῖστον τῶν μακελλευόντων τότε γνωριζομένων.

[2] ἴυλξι of the MS. must be for ἴυγξι.

[3] σφαζομένων is the addition of a later hand in the margin, and scarcely seems to supply the sense required.

the philosophy of oracles,"[1] and learn accurately the record of the things sacrificed, as you read the oracle of Apollo concerning sacrifices,[2] which Porphyry, puffed up with conceit, handed down to his intimates in a mystery, charging them with a terrible oath, as he himself reckoned, that they should not freely tell these things to many. The tragedy of this novel calamity will be well known to you, how the plotting of destroying spirits ruthlessly mangled the human race in various ways, as a flock without a shepherd, coming like an attack of wild wolves from the desert. It was impossible for any one to breathe freely, or to be quiet, but everything was forced together, from one end of heaven to the other, as though by a staff or a thunderbolt. If a man was crossing the sea, he let slip a sacrifice; if he was journeying by land, he sacrificed four-footed beasts. If he were hollowing a cave or digging a piece of land, he threw down a sacrifice to the powers below, and many, by way of buying off their own death, buried some of their own stock while still alive. At any rate, Amistra, the wife of King Xerxes, sent fourteen boys down to Hades alive every year on her own behalf, by covering them with a mound, by way of appeasing the demons of the earth. Stakes and goads and snares had filled the world everywhere; neither air nor land, island nor sea were inopportune for their plottings; but a girdle of guile had encircled the inhabited world, a dark veil of ignorance had enveloped it, and it was not possible for a man to live without trouble and fear. Life was full of suspicion, conditions were unreal, the very fact of chance was affected.

Since therefore the world was full of disorder, and the greater part of life was devoted to demons, he proclaims to those who wish for a brighter[3] life, that they must loathe the table of demons, lest perchance they

[1] This was a book by Porphyry, called περὶ τῆς ἐκ λογίων φιλοσοφίας. It is lost, but is mentioned by Fabricius, v. p. 744. See Introd., p. xiv., for the argument which the reference to this book affords, as against Harnack's belief that the writer of these objections is Porphyry himself.
[2] For this see Euseb., *Praepar. Evang.* iv. 8, 9.
[3] εὐαγέστερον—perhaps "purer."

should at all corrupt the habit of the soul by their fellowship. And again, perceiving how impossible it was for any one who was clothed with flesh to renounce the daily life of the body, he gives permission by way of dispensation, and solemnly counsels them to respect the common market of the shambles and to get their victuals from it. For the matter did not call for trouble, and involved no blame for meddling with such things, seeing that those who undertook the business of the shambles were the ministers of a general and public means of diet. But there were certain servants of temples, picked out and separated from the rest, who in some kind of mystery poured out libations to images and sacrificed with a kind of mystic witchcraft. From these he bids them keep away, and not to touch them at all.

But he destroys the ignorant bounds of Greek belief, cuts their doctrine in pieces, and makes their judgment void, when he says, " An idol is nothing in the world." For the Greeks found out the naming of idols, as the serpent found out the naming of gods; but the judgment of truth does not lay down such an opinion at all. Therefore it is impossible that the theory or standard of idols should be preserved in the world. For the making of images is reasonably spoken of as images, not as idols. These figures, fashioned from gold, silver, bronze, and iron, are silver and gold, but not idols. And the dead bodies of living creatures exist as dead bodies, not as idols. Souls that are loosed from bodies are rightly souls, but not idols. But the representations in statuary of those who are called heroes are images, not idols. And the things that are skilfully painted in colours on tablets, are the delineation of bodies, but certainly not idols. And the things that are called appearances of visions are phantoms and shadows of dreams, but they are not idols. So the great Apostle speaks truth when he says, " An idol is nothing in the world." Unless perchance some one is mad enough to wish to call the elements idols, but he is refuted as he says it; for fire, water, air, and earth are not idols, but properly fire, water, air, and earth.

To what then do those men sacrifice who pay respect to idols? To demons, not to idols; but he does not wish them to be partakers of demons and partakers of Christ. Those who sell food in the shambles do not act as butchers for demons, but for the common life of men, and the end they set before them is not witchcraft but profit, which neither ruins nor corrupts the man who eats. This is the answer to your problem, which you may readily be learning.

CHAPTER XXXVI. Objection based on S. Paul's words about virginity (1 Tim. iv. 1, and 1 Cor. vii. 25).

In his epistles we find another saying like these, where he praises virginity, and then turns round and writes, "In the latter times some shall depart from the faith, giving heed to seducing spirits, forbidding to marry and commanding to abstain from meats" (1 Tim. iv. 1 and 3). And in the Epistle to the Corinthians he says, "But concerning virgins I have no commandment of the Lord" (1 Cor. vii. 25). Therefore he that remains single does not do well, nor will he that refrains from marriage as from an evil thing lead the way in obedience, since they have not a command from Jesus concerning virginity.[1] And how is it that certain people boast of their virginity as if it were some great thing, and say that they are filled with the Holy Ghost similarly to her who was the mother of Jesus?

But we will now cease our attack on Paul, knowing what a battle of the giants he arms against him by his language. But if you are possessed of any resources for replying to these questions, answer without delay.

CHAPTER XLIII. Answer to the objection based on S. Paul's words about virginity (1 Tim. iv. 1, and 1 Cor. vii. 25).

[Here, as always, the context must be studied. Often in Paul's writings a phrase by itself may suggest what he

[1] The word applies to men as well as women, and it is the masculine plural which is here used, but the translation "virginity" best accords with the words which follow about the Blessed Virgin.

did not mean, as when he says, "On whom he will he hath mercy, and whom he will he hardeneth," a statement which must be taken in conjunction with his words about Him "that willeth that all men should be saved." In this passage (from 1 Corinthians) about virgins, it is not clear at once why he should say, "I have no commandment of the Lord, yet I give my judgment as one that hath obtained mercy," seeing that he had Christ speaking within him. The explanation is as follows :—

Virginity is a difficult and unnatural state, and so it is left to the individual to choose it. If Christ forced it on people by a command, they might say that the fault was His if it led to a fall. In simpler matters Christ does give a command through Paul, such as theft, adultery, slander, etc. The wisdom of all this is obvious, and to make virginity a free choice only exalts its position. There is praise for the man who does as he is commanded, but for this act of free-will beyond what is obligatory there is a higher glory.[1] Note that Paul's words show a humble reverence for what he speaks of, for he gives his opinion "as one that hath obtained mercy," not as an Apostle, nor as "judging angels" (but here the virgins are angels in his judgment).

When he says that "There shall arise certain having their conscience seared with a hot iron,"[2] it is because he knew that such heretics would attract men by guile in recommending so excellent a thing as virginity,[3] and thus using a branding-iron of godliness for their own deceitful purposes. These "seared" heresiarchs are like makers of counterfeit coin, washing over their worthless creed with the fine gold of virginity.[4] They are

[1] Macarius reflects the attitude of his age in regarding virginity as a cause of "merit."

[2] 1 Tim. iv. 2. This is the passage quoted in the objection, but v. 2 was then omitted, and only vv. 1 and 3 given. (ἀναστήσονται is not S. Paul's word, but is incorrectly borrowed from the ἀποστήσονται of the previous verse.) These are the men who should "forbid to marry" and therefore commend virginity.

[3] Our apologist is on the wrong track, but it leads to many things of interest to us.

[4] This sentence represents the previous paragraph, but best fits into the argument here.

BOOK III. XLIII

"seared" because they know neither the dew of the Spirit nor the water of baptism, but are scorched at the Chaldean furnace.[1] They insult creation and abuse the creatures of God which He meant to be received with thanksgiving.[2]]

Representatives of these have spread abroad in the children of the Manichæans.[3] Such heresies does the country of the Pisidians contain, and of the Isaurians; Cilicia also, and Lycaonia and all Galatia. Their names it is irksome to repeat; for they are called Encratites and Apotactites, and Eremites,[4] not Christians. They are not seekers of protection from the grace of heaven, but rebels and wanderers from the faith of the Gospel, though, by their abstention from meats, they say that they raise the citadel of godliness. At the head of their chorus doubtless stands Dositheus,[5] a Cilician by race, who confirms their teaching in the course of eight whole books, and magnifies his case by the splendour of his language, saying again and again that marriage is an illegal act, and quite contrary to law. Here are his words, "Through union the world had its beginning; through abstention from it,[6] it would fain have its completion." He says that the tasting of wine and the partaking of flesh is disgusting and loathsome altogether, thus

---

[1] This seems to refer to the fiery furnace of Nebuchadnezzar.

[2] He is referring to the further words of 1 Tim. iv. 3, "abstaining from meats," as well as "forbidding to marry."

[3] The followers of Manes are first found in Asia Minor, as here stated; their system being founded on the theory of a god of good and a god of evil, which was to be found in the religion of Persia. For a further mention of Manes see Bk. IV. ch. xv.

[4] The Encratites (as the name implies) were the Gnostics whose contempt for matter showed itself in their strict asceticism, while the name Apotactites suggests the licentious tendencies of the Antinomian Gnostics, who showed their contempt in the opposite way. The Eremites were ascetics of the deserts.

[5] Dositheus cannot be the head of the Samaritan sect mentioned by Hegesippus (ap. Euseb., *H.E.* iv. 22) and represented in the Clementine writings as the disciple of John the Baptist. Macarius is alone in mentioning him (see also iv. 15, p. 128, l. 24), which shows that this list is not a copy of that of Epiphanius, as Salmon suggested, *D.C.B.*, art. "Macarius."

[6] ἐγκράτεια, the word from which Encratite is derived.

indeed ruthlessly lifting up a cruel branding-iron for those that delight[1] in him. By such reasoning all creation is accursed according to him, all life is under suspicion and hurtful to everybody. Wherefore such men have come into conflict with the Divine, by insulting the beauty of the things that have been created; and nowhere have they benefited the common weal in anything, even though they do teach men to observe virginity, and set self-control as the highest point in life.

The Apostle therefore, knowing all this, protected the Church's doctrine before the time came, to prevent its admitting the attempts of heretical branding-irons. Here you will please conclude the discussion of all these questions. If there is anything which perplexes you again, we will meet and have another discussion, at the convenience of our leisure, with readiness on the part of him who comes off best.[2]

[1] τερπομένοις is the reading suggested by Blondel for MS. προμένοις or ποθομένοις.

[2] If σὺν εὐμαρείᾳ τοῦ κρείττονος is to be so rendered.

BOOK IV

Proem (introducing the first ten questions by the
Philosopher).

WHEN a large number of points had been raised by
the judgment of my Greek opponent, and we had made
clear the obscurity that was in them by means of
much sweat and labour and toil, the philosopher plainly
marked out, so to speak, this fourth contest, for which,
even with your help, Theosthenes,[1] we scarcely took
heart.[2] But what argument it contained I must now
relate.

When no small company was again gathered together,
but a large and distinguished one, as though his intention was purposely to perplex us by the sight of so
many persons, he began to rend in pieces the apostolic
judgment, to the accompaniment of much laughter,
saying as follows:—

THE CHRISTIAN

(Introduction to the answers of Macarius to the
objections of Chapters I to X.)

After all this boasting and terribleness of speech, the
ears of those who stood by were full of fear, and the
understanding of our chosen witnesses was contracted.
We, perceiving the canon of the New Testament thus
trampled underfoot, were smitten in mind and sick in
soul, and troubled in every bodily sense, so that we almost

[1] Theosthenes seems to have been the friend to whom he dedicated
the *Apocriticus*, as well as his supporter during the disputations. If
the whole situation is a fictitious one, the name may have been
suggested by that of Theophilus in S. Luke's dedication. Cf.
Proem to Book III.

[2] Possibly this is a reminiscence of the Homeric use of the words,
as in the passage θάρσει τόνδε γ' ἄεθλον (*Od.* 8. 197).

said, "Lord, save us, we perish." Encircled by so great a storm of cunning devices, but encouraged by some unseen assistance, we stood facing the hurricane which came down upon us, making the Holy Spirit our ally against the face of it. Then, like men rowing in a boat, we began to ply the oars of our tongue and hastened to smite the first of the waves.

CHAPTER I. Objection based on S. Paul's saying that "the fashion of this world passeth away" (1 Cor. vii. 31).

What does Paul mean by saying that the fashion of the world[1] passes away? And how is it possible for them that have to be as though they had not,[2] and they that rejoice as though they rejoiced not, and how can the other old-wives' talk be credible? For how is it possible for him that has to become as though he had not? And how is it credible that he who rejoices should be as though he rejoiced not? Or how can the fashion of this world pass away? What is it that passes away, and why does it do so? For if the Creator[3] were to make it pass away He would incur the charge of moving and altering that which was securely founded. Even if He were to change the fashion into something better, in this again He stands condemned, as not having realised at the time of creation a fitting and suitable fashion for the world, but having created it incomplete, and lacking the better arrangement. In any case, how is one to know that it is into what is good that the world would change if it came to an end late in time? And what benefit is there in the order of phenomena being changed? And if the condition of the visible world is gloomy and a cause for grief, in this, too, the Creator

[1] He leaves out the word "this," in which Macarius follows him.

[2] He is quoting the verses which precede the words about the world passing away, but he omits the word "wives" after "them that have," and is led thereby to make the strange suggestion that God is the subject, and what He has is the world.

[3] δημιουργός, a familiar name as the world-maker of the Gnostic systems.

hears the sound of protest,[1] being reduced to silence
by the sound of reasonable charges[1] against Him, in that
He contrived the parts of the earth in grievous fashion,
and in violation of the reasonableness of nature, and
afterwards repented, and decided to change the whole.

Perchance Paul by this saying teaches him that has,
to be minded as though he had not, in the sense that
the Creator, having the world, makes the fashion of it
pass away, as though He had it not. And he says that
he that rejoices does not rejoice, in the sense that the
Creator is not pleased when He looks upon the fair
and beautiful thing He has created, but, as being much
grieved over it, He formed the plan of transferring and
altering it. So then let us pass over this trivial saying
with mild laughter.

CHAPTER XI. Answer to the objection based on S. Paul's
saying that "the fashion of this world passeth away"
(1 Cor. vii. 31).

[Truly there is a "passing away" for the cloud of your
cunning imagination as well as for the fashion of the
world! "The fashion of the world" may be understood
in many ways. For example, it may mean our transitory
life, or the bodily variation in the different ages of men.
Or, again, as "fashion" means "appearance," it may be
used of a man's shadow, which disappears as soon as the
sun goes in. Even so is "the fashion of the world" a
passing appearance.

"The fashion of the world" also refers to the deceit-
fulness of things human, be they honours or kingdoms
or what you will. In a day a man may pass from a
palace to a dungeon, and in this sense he that hath, and
that rejoiceth, must be as he that doth not. (Of course
there are also changes of the opposite kind, such as
from the dunghill to luxury.) We may find instances
of such "passing away" in Crœsus, dethroned by Cyrus,

[1] It is impossible to reproduce his metaphor. Both words suggest that musical instruments are played so loudly as to make
speaking impossible, viz. καταψάλλεται and καταυλούμενος.

and in Cyrus, conquered by Tomyris. Or look on Babylon, the capital of Assyria, once so fair and of such enormous proportions,[1] then desolated by the Persians, and now not preserving a trace of its former greatness. Or the once all-powerful Macedonian nation, now absorbed in the Roman Empire. And it is superfluous to record how many local rulers have evaporated like smoke, or how many women who were queens have perished,[2] or of how many famous men the glory has departed.

The change in "the fashion of the world" is clearly seen in the seasons. The spring with all its beauty yields to scorching summer. Soon the time of ripe fruit hastens on to autumn, and then comes the winter, in which we are now,[3] to take away our joy. Yes, all things change, even as the sea never maintains a perpetual calm.

If you wish to make out that things do *not* change, you must also show that they are uncreated, for it is only that which has no beginning that can be without an end. And if you think human things do not "pass away," you necessarily make them everlasting! Why, even an uncivilised Scythian would tell you the difference between what is uncreated and lasting, and what is created and passing away.

Paul therefore rightly added: "Let not him that rejoiceth rejoice," for the object of his rejoicing soon passes. Even day and night are uncertain; the day may be bright or stormy, and there is no fixed hour at which the night begins, but sometimes it is ten hours long, sometimes twelve.

---

[1] Details of the measurements of the city are given, which suggest that the writer was familiar with that part of the world.

[2] The obvious reference seems to be to Zenobia, Queen of Palmyra, and her defeat by Aurelius. This would be a matter of recent history to the opponent of Macarius, if he dates from the beginning of the fourth century. Does it suggest that the answer was of the same date?

[3] This is a very natural touch, and it is more easy to connect it with an actual disputation than merely with the writing of a book.

CHAPTER II. Objection based on the saying of S. Paul that "we which are alive shall be caught up in the clouds" (1 Thess. iv. 15–17).

Let us consider another wise remark of his, astounding and perverted, wherein he says, "We which are alive and remain, shall not go before them that are asleep unto the coming of the Lord, for the Lord himself shall descend from heaven with a shout, with the voice of the archangel, and with the trump of God; and the dead in Christ shall rise first: then we which are alive shall be caught up together with them in a cloud, to meet the Lord in the air: and so shall we ever be with the Lord" (1 Thess. iv. 15–17).[1] Here is a thing that indeed rises in the air and shoots up to heaven, an enormous and far-reaching lie. This, when recited to the beasts without understanding, causes even them to bellow and croak out their sounding din in reply, when they hear of men in the flesh flying like birds in the air, or carried on a cloud. For this boast is a mighty piece of quackery, that living things, pressed down by the burden of physical bulk, should receive the nature of winged birds, and cross the wide air like some sea, using the cloud as a chariot. Even if such a thing is possible, it is monstrous, and apart from all that is suitable. For nature which created all things[2] from the beginning appointed places befitting the things which were brought into being, and ordained that each should have its proper sphere, the sea for the water creatures, the land for those of the dry ground, the air for winged creatures, and the higher atmosphere for heavenly bodies. If one of these were moved from its proper abode, it would disappear on arrival in a strange condition and abode. For instance, if you wanted to take a creature of the

[1] He places too late the words "unto the coming of the Lord," and omits "and remain" after the second occurrence of "we which are alive." "Cloud" for "clouds" is another unimportant inaccuracy.

[2] He does not intend to substitute an impersonal power for the Creator; indeed, further on he attributes creation to the Word of God.

water and force it to live on the dry land, it is readily destroyed and dies. Again, if you throw a land animal of a dry kind into the water, it will be drowned. And if you cut off a bird from the air, it will not endure it, and if you remove a heavenly body from the upper atmosphere, it will not stand it. Neither has the divine and active Word of God done this, nor ever will do it, although He is able to change the lot of the things that come into being. For He does not do and purpose anything according to His own ability, but according to its suitability He preserves things, and keeps the law of good order. So, even if He is able to do so, He does not make the earth to be sailed over, nor again does He make the sea to be ploughed or tilled; nor does He use His power in making virtue into wickedness nor wickedness into virtue, nor does He adapt a man to become a winged creature, nor does He place the stars below and the earth above.

Wherefore we may reasonably declare that it is full of twaddle to say that men will ever be caught up into the air.

And Paul's lie becomes very plain when he says, "We which are alive." For it is three hundred years since he said this,[1] and no body has anywhere been caught up, either Paul's or any one else's. So it is time this saying of Paul became silent, for it is driven away in confusion.

CHAPTER XII. Answer to the objection based on S. Paul's words that "we which are alive shall be caught up in the clouds" (1 Thess. iv. 15–17).

[We must act as reasoning beings, and look for a mystic meaning in the words. He means that at Christ's second coming the godly will be caught up from the corruption of this life. Just as the water in the sea is heavy, and yet is drawn up into the air in clouds, so shall man be drawn up by angelic might. For the "cloud," which is sometimes high and sometimes near the earth, signifies the angels, who both rise to heaven and descend to earth in the course of their service. For this we may

---

[1] See Introd., p. xvii.

refer to Abbakum,[1] drawn up by a cloud from Judæa, and carried and set down over the Babylonian pit, or to the angels which Jacob saw ascending and descending. The prophets also show angels to be clouds, as when Isaiah says (xv. 6), "I will command the clouds not to rain upon the vine," *i.e.* the angels are not to rain visions upon Israel. Again Daniel says (vii. 13) that Christ will come "with the clouds of heaven," while Christ said He would come and all the angels with Him (Matt. xxv. 31).

Also the Psalms speak of "Clouds and darkness round about him" (Ps. xcvii. 2), where His judgment-seat is the severity of the law, which will be combined with the grace of the Gospel (cf. Ps. civ. 3). Also the Gospel says, "He shall send forth his angels and gather the elect from the four winds of heaven" (Mark xiii. 26, 27).

That it was the Apostle's habit to allegorise thus, may be seen from such pasages as "The night is far spent, the day is at hand."

At the end of the world, it is the trumpet of angelic voices which will sound, and give man the power to rise, just as the horses of fire, which were really angels, took up Elijah.

With regard to your argument that everything must remain in its own element, mark that it is not by remaining in themselves, but in something different, that created things are preserved. You cannot keep fire in fire, but in the air. What is wet is kept in what is dry, as water in a vessel, etc. The same applies to things light and heavy, and to soul and body.

And mark further that things are only what they are, relatively to something else. For example, there would be no test of an unrighteous man if there were no righteousness. So it is not strange that angels should draw men up just as clouds draw water. (For the identification of men with water, see Isaiah xvii. 13, "Behold many nations as water.")

There is no falsehood in Paul declaring that "*We*

[1] The story is taken from the Apocryphal part of Daniel, viz. xiv. 34-36 (Bel and the Dragon). The LXX gives the name as Αμβακούμ, in A.V. Habbacuc.

shall be caught up," although the resurrection did not take place in his day, for he is very fond of identifying his own humanity with that of the whole race.

CHAPTER III. Objection based on S. Matthew's words that the Gospel should be preached in all the world (Matt. xxiv. 14).[1]

We must mention also that saying which Matthew gave us, in the spirit of a slave who is made to bend himself in a mill-house, when he said, "And the gospel of the kingdom shall be preached in all the world, and then shall the end come."[2] For lo, every quarter of the inhabited world has experience of the Gospel, and all the bounds and ends of the earth possess it complete,[3] and nowhere is there an end, nor will it ever come.

So let this saying only be spoken in a corner!

CHAPTER XIII. Answer to the objection based on S. Matthew's words that the Gospel should be preached in all the world (Matt. xxiv. 14).

[The word "end" may be used in more senses than one; for example, the end of war is peace, and the end of ignorance is knowledge. And so the end of wickedness is godliness. This is exactly the end which has come about through the preaching of the Gospel. So that they who once in their ignorance served idols' temples, now in the light of knowledge serve God as temples of the Holy Spirit. And therefore, in this

[1] The abbreviated form of the quotation is tacitly accepted by Macarius in his answer.

[2] It is very remarkable that, wherever it is possible, the attack is made on Christ's followers, and not on Himself. Here it is only the Evangelist who is blamed for words which are attributed to Christ. See Introd., p. xv.

[3] The previous objection has stated that only 300 years have passed, so that this cannot have been written later than the early part of the fourth century. To speak thus is therefore an exaggeration, as Macarius shows in his answer. But it is very significant that a heathen should regard Christianity as universally spread, even before it became a lawful religion.

BOOK IV. III, XIII

sense, an "end" has come to the tragic side of the world.

But if we take the ordinary meaning of "end," we may say, first, that it is even now close at the doors; and secondly, that the Gospel has not yet been preached everywhere. Seven races of the Indians who live in the desert in the south-east have not received it;[1] nor the Ethiopians who are called Macrobians,[2] dwelling in the south-west, at the mouth of the ocean. These may be described as "Having laws that no one should wrong or be wronged by another, drinking milk and eating flesh, living for something like a hundred and fifty years, and never diseased or weakly until the end." Then, of course, there are in the west both the Maurusians and those who dwell beyond the great northern river Ister, which is gathered from five-and-thirty streams, and, carrying countless merchant vessels on its broad and constant stream, shuts off the country of the Scythians, where twelve tribes of nomad barbarians live, of whose savage state Herodotus tells us, and their evil customs derived from their ancestors. But the Gospel must "be preached for a witness unto all (nations)" before the end comes.

When all men have heard it, then great will be the punishment of those who reject it. And so God in His mercy delays the revolution of time which brings the end. This He does without real alteration of His will. Even the human mind can now make a triangle into a square and a square into a triangle without altering the size, and therefore God can, without changing the sum total of time, make one day to be a thousand years, and a thousand years to be one day.[3] So we must find no

[1] The way he locates these races gives some clue to the place of writing. See Introd., p. xxi.

[2] These are also referred to in iii. 15 (see p. 79). Their name implies that they were "long-lived."

[3] This is probably a reference to 2 Peter iii. 8, but not necessarily so, as it may refer only to Ps. xc. 4. It is curious that elsewhere Macarius ignores 2 Peter when its use was to be expected. See Introd., p. xxv. His very involved statement comes to this in the end, but it begins with the awkward words οὕτως ἔτη τὴν ἡμέραν ἐργάζεται χίλια καὶ τὴν ἡμέραν οὐ πολλὰς ἀλλ' ἔχειν μίαν ἡμέραν.

difficulty in this lengthening of the time. It is for us and for our benefit that the end has not yet come.]

CHAPTER IV. Objection based on the divine assurance given to both S. Paul and S. Peter, and their martyrdom in spite of it.

Let us look at what was said to Paul, "The Lord spoke to Paul in the night by a vision, Be not afraid, but speak, for I am with thee, and no man shall set on thee to hurt thee" (Acts xviii. 9–10). And yet no sooner was he seized in Rome than this fine fellow, who said that we should judge angels, had his head cut off.[1] And Peter again, who received authority to feed the lambs, was nailed to a cross and impaled on it.[2] And countless others, who held opinions like theirs, were either burnt, or put to death by receiving some kind of punishment or maltreatment. This is not worthy of the will of God, nor even of a godly man, that a multitude of men should be cruelly punished through their relation to His own grace and faith, while the expected resurrection and coming remains unknown.

CHAPTER XIV. Answer to the objection based on the divine assurance given to both S. Paul and S. Peter, and their martyrdom in spite of it.

[In each case the martyrdom came after the struggle of life was over, and the great work of bringing souls to Christ in many lands had been fulfilled.

Such an end to their life meant a higher fame. The highest honour is for soldiers who defend their country against the enemy to the death. So, after having marshalled the faithful all over the world into Christ's army, and stayed the fierceness of the enemy from the

---

[1] He thus echoes the Christian tradition that S. Paul was beheaded at Rome, but he shows the same desire to put his martyrdom at an impossibly early moment as in the case of S. Peter.

[2] In iii. 22 he uses similar language about S. Peter's crucifixion, which he strangely places within a few months of his being charged to feed the lambs.

BOOK IV. IV, XIV, V

rest, they won an unfading crown, and encouraged many to win it likewise. A violent death was a seal upon their life, and proved the greatness of their zeal.[1]

During their work both Peter and Paul were many times protected by their Lord from the plots of the Jews, but when the seeds of their faith had taken root, He granted them the final glory of martyrdom. In thus treating His soldiers, God acted as a wise general, for many were hostile, and might have ascribed their works to magic had they died an ordinary death, or vanished from before tribunals.[2] To conquer torments by enduring to the end was their best answer to these.

Some paltry critics are prepared to find fault with the saints in either case. If they are protected from death, these would assert that they would never have endured to the end. If they face it to the end, they would say that it proved they were not really righteous men. And so God, in His love for His saints, sometimes rescues them from death, as in the case of Daniel and the three children, and sometimes lets them witness by their death that they are neither cowards nor hypocrites, as in the case of Peter and Paul.]

CHAPTER V. Objection based on Christ's words that many should come in His name, saying, I am Christ (Matt. xxiv. 4, 5).

And there is another dubious little saying which one may manifestly take hold of, when Christ says: "Take heed that no man deceive you; for many shall come in my name, saying, I am Christ, and shall deceive many." And behold! three hundred years have passed by, and even more, and no one of the kind has anywhere appeared. Unless indeed you are going to adduce

[1] He adds that they also beat thereby the seed of the dragon, for by being beheaded Paul lured the serpent to greediness for blood and milk, while Peter beat him with his cross. For the legend of milk flowing from S. Paul's wound, see Introd., p. xxvi.
[2] Apollonius of Tyana is here intended. He was mentioned by name, and this same incident referred to, in iii. 8. See also below, in the next objection.

Apollonius of Tyana,[1] a man who was adorned with all philosophy. But you would not find another. Yet it is not concerning one but concerning many that He says that such shall arise.

CHAPTER XV. Answer to the objection based on Christ's words that many should come in His name, saying, I am Christ (Matt. xxiv. 4, 5).

[You only speak thus from ignorance. I can tell you of many men who in Christ's name deceived many, and finally deceived themselves to their ruin.]

At once then I can tell you of Manes in Persia, who imitated the name of Christ, and corrupted by his error many a satrapy and many a country in the East, and up to this day pollutes the world by creeping over it with his injurious seed.[2] And another is Montanus in Phrygia, who, bearing this name, underwent in the name of the Lord an ascetic and unnatural course of life, revealing himself as the abode of a baneful demon, and feeding on his error through all the land of Mysia as far as that of Asia. And so great was the power of the hidden demon which lurked within him, that he very nearly tainted the whole world with the poison of his error. And why should I tell you of Cerinthus and Simon, or Marcion or Bardesanes,[3] or Droserius[4] or Dositheus the Cilician,[5] or countless others whose number I shrink from reckoning. All these and those who affected them, appropriating to themselves the name of Christianity, wrought unspeakable error in the world, and have taken numberless spoils and captives. Moreover, as these are Anti-

[1] See note on iii. 1. p. 52.
[2] Harnack has used this as an argument for the late date of the *Apocriticus*. But as early as A.D. 290 the Manichæans had so spread in Africa that the Proconsul of Africa was ordered to burn the leaders with their books.
[3] The Syrian Gnostic, who was born at Edessa in A.D. 155.
[4] Droserius appears in the dialogue called Adamantius (Pseudo-Origen). In Bk. IV. Droserius is made to suggest the Valentinian origin of evil, and is answered by Adamantius.
[5] Dositheus appears again in a similar list in iii. 43, p. 115, l. 16, where interesting details are given. He is not otherwise known to us.

BOOK IV. xv, vi

christs, or contrary to God, their followers are no longer willing to bear the name of Christian, but like to be called, after the name of their leaders, Manichæans, Montanists, Marcionists, Droserians, and Dositheans. Do you see the baneful armies of many Antichrists terribly inflamed against Christ and the Christians, and then do you say that none of the things has come of which the Saviour prophesied? Do you behold the armed array of those contrary to God, and then do you set aside the Saviour's prediction? It is not right to do so, but rather to assent to what was said by Him. So much for this objection.]

CHAPTER VI. Objection based on the saying about the Day of Judgment in the Apocalypse of Peter.[1]

By way of giving plenty of such sayings, let me quote also what was said in the Apocalypse of Peter. He thus introduces the statement that the heaven will be judged together with the earth. "The earth shall present all men to God in the day of judgment, itself too being about to be judged, together with the heaven which contains it." No one is so uneducated or so stupid as not to know that the things which have to do with earth are subject to disturbance, and are not naturally such as to preserve their order, but are uneven; whereas the things in heaven have an order which remains perpetually alike, and always goes on in the same way, and never suffers alteration, nor indeed will it ever do so. For it stands as God's most exact piece of workmanship. Wherefore it is impossible that the things should be undone which are worthy of a better fate, as being fixed by a divine ordinance which cannot be touched.

And why will heaven be judged? Will it some day be shown to have committed some sin, though it preserves the order which from the beginning was approved by God, and abides in sameness always? Unless indeed some one will address the Creator, slanderously asserting

[1] Macarius in chapter xvi. combines this question with the next in his answer.

I

that heaven is deserving of judgment, as having allowed the judge to speak any portents against it which are so wondrous and so great.[1]

CHAPTER VII. Objection based on the similar words in Isaiah about the heaven being rolled up as a scroll (Isa. xxxiv. 4).

And it[2] makes this statement again, which is full of impiety, saying: "And all the might of heaven shall be dissolved, and the heaven shall be rolled together as a scroll, and all the stars shall fall as leaves from a vine, and as leaves fall from a fig tree." And another boast is made in portentous falsehood and monstrous quackery: "Heaven and earth shall pass away, but my words shall not pass away" (Matt. xxiv. 35). For, pray, how could any one say that the words of Jesus would stand, if heaven and earth no longer existed? Moreover, if Christ were to do this and bring heaven down, He would be imitating the most impious of men, even those who destroy their own children. For it is acknowledged by the Son that God is Father of heaven and earth when He says: "Father, Lord of heaven and earth" (Matt. xi. 25). And John the Baptist magnifies heaven and declares that the divine gifts of grace are sent from it, when he says: "A man can do[3] nothing, except it be given him from heaven" (John iii. 27). And the prophets[4] say that heaven is the holy habitation of God, in the words: "Look down from thy holy habitation,[5] and bless thy people Israel" (Deut. xxvi. 15).

If heaven, which is so great and of such importance

---

[1] This is an attempt to translate οὐρανὸν . . . ὡς τὸν κριτὴν ἀνασχόμενον κατ' αὐτοῦ τινα τερατεύεσθαι οὕτω θαυμαστὸν, οὕτω μεγάλα (reading θαυμαστά).

[2] He seems to think he is again quoting from the Apocalypse of Peter, though the word used is neuter. He gives no hint that he is quoting the Old Testament, but Macarius passes over the reference to an Apocryphal book in the previous question, as of doubtful authority, and proceeds to quote this as from Isaiah.

[3] This is a misquotation for "receive."

[4] The quotation is really from the law.

[5] He strangely omits the very word most needed, *i. e.* "heaven."

in the witness borne to it, shall pass away, what shall be the seat thereafter of Him who rules over it? And if the element of earth perishes, what shall be the footstool of Him who sits there, for He[1] says: "The heaven is my throne, and the earth is the footstool of my feet." So much for the passing away of heaven and earth.

CHAPTER XVI. Answer to the two objections based on the words of the Apocalypse of Peter and of Isaiah concerning the passing away of heaven and earth.

[It is plain that the passing away of heaven and earth is through no fault of theirs, and equally plain that it must be accepted as a scriptural fact. For even if we pass over the Apocalypse of Peter,[2] we are brought to the same thing by the other two passages—by Isaiah xxxiv. 4: "The heavens shall be rolled together as a scroll, and all the stars shall fall, as leaves fall from a vine, and as leaves fall from a fig tree"; and by Matthew xxiv. 35: "Heaven and earth shall pass away, but my words shall not pass away."

All the rest of creation was created, not for its own sake, but for man's sake. Man alone was created for his own sake, that he might glorify the wisdom of Him who made him. Not that such glorifying adds to God's glory, any more than for a man to warm himself adds to the warmth of the fire. So man gives God nothing new, but makes himself part of God by his union with the Godhead.[3] So the world was like a great house made for man to live in. But soon he failed to be what the Creator made him, and in utter folly fell and was corrupted with regard to divine things. God therefore

[1] As he has made no previous reference to Isaiah, it would seem that the words are attributed to God.

[2] With this cursory mention Macarius passes on from the words of that Apocryphal book, as quoted in the first objection he is answering (chapter vi.), and proceeds to Isaiah's similar words, adduced without acknowledgment in chapter vii. It is evident that he regarded this Apocalypse as quite outside the canon.

[3] ἑαυτὸν ἀποθεοῖ κοινωνῶν τῇ θεότητι.

resolved to send him to another place through death, in order that, after a separation from the flesh which covered him, he might again bring it to incorruptibility. So, when the master was removed from the house, that house was obliged to undergo what had not been intended for it. Just as it is right for the keeper of a vineyard only to let his tent remain until the fruit is plucked, and then he says farewell to his tent, and also to the beauty of the vineyard, so must the beauty of heaven and earth be lost, as soon as the reasoning essence [1] of man, which abides in the world as in a tent, departs to its own appointed place, when the fruit of righteousness has everywhere been plucked.[2]

Thus the world's splendour will be of no more use when man is gone. And yet as man will pass through death into a better and incorruptible state, so will it be with all the world. It will be like a damaged silver vessel, which the artificer melts down, and then makes a new and better one of it. It passes away, but the "Logos"[3] of it remains with the artificer. Just so Christ says His "Logos"[4] will remain when heaven and earth have passed away. Therefore all created things will in this way have a second and a better beginning.[5]

There is a deep meaning in the prophet's words "as leaves fall from a vine or a fig tree." For the fall of the leaves looks like the end of the life of the tree, but it is really the advance to something better. His purpose in choosing out these two particular trees may be either because, owing to careful husbandry, they only cast their leaves once (a type of God's care for His universe), or because, in speaking of the world passing away because

---

[1] λογικὴ οὐσία.

[2] This excellent passage well carries on the simile suggested by Isaiah.

[3] This is in accordance with the Platonic theory of ideas. λόγος is perhaps best rendered "rationale," but the original word must be kept for the sake of the play on the words in this sentence.

[4] This is a strangely forced interpretation of the passage in Matt. xxiv. 35.

[5] In this statement he passes in his philosophising from Platonism to Origenism.

BOOK IV. XVI, VIII 133

of man's sin, it is appropriate to mention the fig, which was the first mark of Adam's fall, in the apron which he made; and the vine, which marked Noah's shame.

There is also a mystic meaning in his words, "The heaven shall be rolled up as a scroll." For the heavenly book of Christ's earthly life was now closed to the disciples, and will only be opened again afresh when man is freed from the decay of this life.

You ask where God's seat will be when His throne and His footstool have passed away. The prophet's words were really meant to make us realise the greatness of One whose relation to the great universe was such. They do not suggest that God will be affected by the change of these things. Indeed, there are many passages in the Psalms (*e.g.* cii. 25–27) to prove that God's seat is for ever, and certainly He had a habitation before heaven and earth were created. The Psalmist compares them to an old garment rolled up and changed; such indeed is the work of the heavenly fuller.

Yet another allegory underlies the words. Heaven and earth may mean man, in his twofold nature. His soul is the throne of God the Word, and his body, which Christ took, is His footstool. To this mystery the Baptist refers in his words about the latchet of His shoe (Mark i. 7), and the Psalmist when he says, "Fall down before his footstool, for he is holy" (Ps. xcviii. 5). Although the Word said He would dwell in men and walk in them (2 Cor. vi. 16, from Lev. xxvi. 11, 12), yet men have so sinned that they have fallen like stars, and are no longer fit to be His habitation. Accordingly, there must be a new beginning, "a new heaven and a new earth" (Isa. lxv. 17).]

CHAPTER VIII. Objection based on the comparisons of the grain of mustard seed, etc. (Matt. xiii. 31–33 and 45, 46).

Let us touch on another piece of teaching even more fabulous than this, and obscure as night, contained in the words, "The kingdom of heaven is like unto a grain of mustard seed"; and again, "The kingdom of heaven is like unto leaven"; and once more, "It is like unto a merchant seeking goodly pearls." These imaginings do not come from (real) men, nor even from women who put their trust in dreams. For when any one has a message to give concerning great and divine matters, he is obliged to make use of common things which pertain to men, in order to make his meaning clear, but not such degraded and unintelligible things as these. These sayings, besides being base and unsuitable to such matters, have in themselves no intelligent meaning or clearness. And yet it was fitting that they should be very clear indeed, because they were not written for the wise or understanding, but for babes.

CHAPTER IX. Objection based on Christ's words about revealing these things unto babes (Matt. xi. 25).[1]

If indeed it was necessary to express that other utterance, as Jesus says, "I thank thee, Father, Lord of heaven and earth, because thou hast hid these things from the wise and prudent, and hast revealed them unto babes," and as it is written in Deuteronomy (xxix. 29), "The hidden things for the Lord our God, and the manifest things for us,"[2] therefore the things that are written for the babes and the ignorant ought to be clearer and not wrapped in riddles. For if the mysteries have been hidden from the wise, and unreasonably poured out to babes and those that give suck, it is better to be desirous of senselessness and ignorance, and this is the great achievement of the wisdom of Him who came to earth, to hide the rays of knowledge from the wise, and to reveal them to fools and babes.

[1] All the answer which Macarius gives to this objection is contained in the last paragraph of chapter xvii., which is his answer to the previous objection of chapter viii.
[2] Eng. Vers. "The secret things belong unto the Lord our God: but those things which are revealed belong unto us."

CHAPTER XVII. Answer to the two objections (Chaps. VIII and IX) based on the comparisons of the grain of mustard seed, etc. (Matt. xiii. 31, etc.), and Christ's words about revealing these things unto babes (Matt. xi. 25).

[Great things are rightly compared with the small things of everyday life. This is just what philosophers do, for to get a conception of our enormous earth in its relation to heaven, they compare it to a mere point, a grain of millet. And even heaven itself was embraced by Aratus of Cilicia [1] in so feeble a thing as a small circle.

Why then should not Christ similarly compare the kingdom of heaven to "leaven"? For it is the small leaven that fits large quantities of meal for man's food, and this is the way the kingdom affects human society. The woman who took the meal is obviously creation, and the "three measures" of it are either present, past, or future; man's body, soul, and spirit; or the three dimensions.

So again with the "grain of mustard seed"; it is hot and pungent, useful both for cleansing and for seasoning food, and also of surprising growth. The kingdom has its counterpart in all this, for it cleanses from evil, warms the understanding, and when sown in the world it uplifts men to holiness. Therefore Christ chose, not a sacred bean like the Greeks,[2] but a mustard seed, to show the cleansing power of the kingdom.

The "pearl" likewise is chosen to show its preciousness. The pearl has a watery dwelling at first, which suggests the lowly dwelling of the Godhead in flesh. Then afterwards the heavenly pearl brings its heavenly brightness to all who obtain it through their good works.

The sayings were thus quite clear, and were for those who were babes only in wickedness, and not in know-

[1] Aratus was a Cilician astronomer. See Introd., p. xxi.
[2] A reference to the Pythagoreans.

ledge of the mysteries. It is against the wisdom of this world that Christ closed His heavenly doctrines.[1]]

CHAPTER X. Objection based on the saying about the sick needing a physician, and not the righteous (Matt. ix. 12; Luke v. 31).

It is right to examine another matter of a much more reasonable kind (I say this by way of contrast), "They that are whole need not a physician, but they that are sick." Christ unravels these things to the multitude about His own coming to earth. If then it was on account of those who are weak, as He Himself says, that He faced sins, were not our forefathers weak, and were not our ancestors diseased with sin? And if indeed those who are whole need not a physician, and He came not to call the righteous but sinners to repentance, so that Paul speaks thus: "Jesus Christ came into the world to save sinners, of whom I am chief" (1 Tim. i. 15); if then this is so, and he that has gone astray is called, and he that is diseased is healed, and the unrighteous is called, but the righteous is not, it follows that he who was neither called nor in need of the healing of the Christians would be a righteous man who had not gone astray. For he who has no need of healing is the man who turns away from the word which is among the faithful, and the more he turns away from it, the more righteous and whole he is, and the less he goes astray.

CHAPTER XVIII. Answer to the objection based on the saying about the sick needing a physician, and not the righteous (Matt. ix. 12; Luke v. 31).

[It is quite plain that in dividing sick and whole, righteous and sinners, Christ is referring to the two kinds of reasonable beings. The "whole" and the "righteous" are the angels, whose pure and uncorruptible nature

---

[1] In this last brief paragraph Macarius answers a further objection, thus curtailing his own chapters for the second time in Book IV.

requires no call to repentance. The "sick" and the "sinners" are the race of men, whose glory was at first equal to the angels, but they fell into the sickness of sin.[1] The Word in pity came down to call and heal them, as we see in His words: "Behold, thou art made whole, sin no more" (John v. 14). He actually mingled Himself with them and with their life, in order to draw them upward, so that He might rejoice over those on earth as well as those in heaven.

His call began directly man had fallen, with the cry, "Adam, where art thou?" It was extended to Cain, Enoch, Noah, Abraham, Moses and the prophets. The angels were already close to Him, so there was no need to call them, but He called men, who were fallen far away. Had men obeyed God's first commands, the Creator would not have become a physician and come down to call them back from disobedience. As it was, He had to cry to one: "What hast thou done?" (Gen. iii. 9); to another, "Come out from thy land" (Gen. xii. 1), etc., calling them to be as Himself.

It is a mistake to suppose that He only called men during His earthly life. Had it been so, He would have said: "I am not here *now* to call the righteous," etc. But the aorist tense "I came" leaves His coming quite undefined, so that it extends from Adam and the Patriarchs onwards.

And if some have refused the call, the fault is in their own choice. The heavenly sun is like the earthly, whose brightness is for all, and yet some who are drunken remain in the darkness.

Let us now be at peace, unless you have some other cause of perplexity to bring forward.]

[1] Thus does Macarius run away from the point, and content himself with an allegorical interpretation.

CHAPTER XIX. Objection based on the saying: "But ye were washed, but ye were sanctified" (1 Cor. vi. 11).

The Philosopher.[1]

He, as though roused from some condition of detachment from the earth, directed against us a saying from Homer, speaking thus with no little laughter: "Rightly did Homer order the manly Greeks to be silent, as they had been trained: he published abroad the wavering sentiment of Hector, addressing the Greeks in measured language, saying, 'Stay, ye Argives; smite not, ye Achæan youths; for Hector of the waving plume is resolved to speak a word.'" Even so we now all sit in quietness here; for the interpreter of the Christian doctrines promises us and surely affirms that he will unravel the dark passages of the Scriptures.

Tell therefore, my good sir, to us who are following what you have to say, what the Apostle means when he says, "But such were some of you" (plainly something base), "but ye were washed, but ye were sanctified, but ye were justified in the name of the Lord Jesus Christ, and in the Spirit of our God" (1 Cor. vi. 11). For we are surprised and truly perplexed in mind at such things, if a man, when once he is washed from so many defilements and pollutions, shows himself to be pure; if by wiping off the stains of so much weakness in his life, fornication, adultery, drunkenness, theft, unnatural vice, poisoning, and countless base and disgusting things, and simply by being baptised and calling on the name of Christ, he is quite easily freed from them, and puts off the whole of his guilt just as a snake puts off his old slough. Who is there who would not, on the strength of these, venture on evil deeds, some mentionable and others not, and do such things as are neither to be uttered in speech nor endured in deeds, in the knowledge that he will receive remission from so many criminal actions only by believing and being baptised, and in the

[1] The following paragraph introduces the next six questions.

BOOK IV. xix, xxv 139

hope that he will after this receive pardon from Him who is about to judge the quick and the dead? These things incline the man who hears them to commit sin, and in each particular he is thus taught to practise what is unlawful. These things have the power to set aside the training of the law, and cause righteousness itself to be of no avail against the unrighteous. They introduce into the world a form of society which is without law, and teach men to have no fear of ungodliness; when a man sets aside a pile of countless wrongdoings simply by being baptised. Such then is the boastful fiction of the saying.

CHAPTER XXV. Answer to the objection based on the saying: "But ye were washed, but ye were sanctified" (1 Cor. vi. 11).

The Christian.[1]

The Greek, by importing such terrible language into his questionings, seemed to be mocking us and casting us into the confusion of perplexity. But we, earnestly imploring in our heart the aid of Him who reveals the deep things of darkness, and makes clear the knowledge of man by His teaching, faced in due season each of the arguments he had spoken. We addressed the band of them thus: "What great themes and how mightily obscure are they in the way you have set them before us! But accept the plain answer to them, since it is Christ that brings you this interpretation through our means. Hearken then first to the first point, and to the second expressed in the second discourse, then to the third likewise, and the fourth and fifth, and again to the sixth question at issue, along with the seventh."[2]

We must therefore speak first of the saying uttered by

[1] The following paragraph is an introduction to the next six answers.
[2] It is only here that Macarius plainly refers to his method of arrangement, taking a number of objections to answer at the same time. The average number is seven, but this is not always strictly adhered to. The odd thing is that in this case the number of questions answered consecutively is only six.

the Apostle : "And such were some of you ; but ye were washed, but ye were sanctified, but ye were justified in the name of our Lord Jesus Christ and in the spirit of our God."

[If the sinful creature is sometimes pitied and freely forgiven by his Creator, it is only what we see in things human. The law may decide that a wrongdoer is to be punished, but the king whose law it is may overrule it by his pardoning grace, even though the man does not deserve it. A reprieve from death has often been given thus. Such grace does not conform to the letter of the law, for, if it did, it would not be grace. There are already many things that God's grace gives us which we have not deserved, such as the light of the sun. Rightly then does he give sinners freedom from their sin, as a father pitying his children. But His deed is made to shine forth as a gift of grace, that it may not be ascribed to their own doing. The law does not join in its Master's gift of grace, but punishes the sin ; and the Lord does not stoop to the level of the law, but simply forgives it.

A true illustration of all this has just occurred. It is not a story of long ago, for it happened only yesterday. Certain obvious criminals, by supplicating the king during his royal progress, obtained a reversal of their sentence, and were let off without any punishment, while certain others, who did not approach him, were condemned, in spite of their obvious innocence of a share in the crimes committed.[1] Why then should the Apostle be blamed in what he says to those who have been "washed" and freed from the penalty that was theirs under the law?

Note that to the words "Ye were washed" he adds "in the name of the Lord." Just as a signature carries weight either in the army or the law-court if it is in the king's hand, and not if it is in men's own, just so the

---

[1] Macarius refers elsewhere to the Emperor as βασιλεύς. Apparently there had just been a "royal progress" in the East in his locality. It may be only a bit of sham realism, or an event which occurred when Macarius was writing his book ; but on the face of it, it seems to give some support to the theory of a real dialogue.

water only has the power to cleanse from the stain of evil when it has been marked by the name of Christ.]

For the naming of the Saviour Jesus, that mystically takes place upon the water, makes it no longer common water, but causes it to be set apart, and indescribably potent to wash away not only that which shows on the visible body, but the very hidden part of the conscience. It is able to furnish the reason with weapons like an army, and to fill with life the man who is washed in it, so that he no longer fears the threatening of the law, which was hanging over the heads of those who are liable to it. For he flees for refuge to the Master of the law Himself, and receives from Him the whole armour of grace, and is thus able to pierce the battle-line of the passions. See then the defence and the array which follows, see the flash of light given by the Apostle's teaching. He does not say at once "Ye were sanctified," but he puts first "Ye were washed"; for first a man is washed and then he is purified, that is to say, sanctified. For as soda when put in water wipes out the dirt, so the name of Christ, when wrapped in the waters, cleanses him who comes to them from his fall, and reveals him shining with the bright light of grace. Then after the sanctification it completes his justification, when every unrighteous deed has been put off.

He says[1] that this does not befall those who are in a state of salvation in any other way than "in the name of the Lord and the Spirit of God." In a way that is inspired and altogether fitting, he laid down the dogma that grace is supplied to the faithful from the Trinity, when he said it was in the name of the Lord and the Spirit,[2] and not only Spirit, but God's Spirit. For he

[1] The passage which begins here, and continues to the end of the paragraph (268 words in the Greek) is the only one where the inner doctrines of the Christian Creed are expounded. It is either a later interpolation, or an exception to the usual style of the book. In the latter case, it is not easy to reconcile with an early date for Macarius. See Introd., pp. xviii and xxviii.

[2] It is to be noted that he here misquotes his text, and assists his argument by reading τοῦ πνεύματος instead of ἐν τῷ πνεύματι, thus making " in the name of" refer to Him as well as to Christ.

thus names the Godhead of the Three, by saying, not
"in the names" but "in the name." For there is one
name of God both upon the Father and the Son and
the Holy Spirit, and God is one in three Persons, and
is so named. The Father does not receive the believer
without the Son, nor does the Son bring any one to
the Father apart from the Spirit. For behold the mystic
sense in which he said, "But ye were washed, but ye
were sanctified, but ye were justified." For the man
whom Jesus has washed, is sanctified by the Spirit.
And the Father justifies him whom the Spirit has
sanctified. This is not because Christ in washing him
cannot sanctify, nor that the Spirit in sanctifying has
not power to justify, nor that the Father in justifying
is too weak to wash or sanctify whomsoever He wills.
For the Father is sufficient both to wash and to sanctify
and to justify all things, and the Son and the Holy
Spirit likewise. But it is fitting that the Son, as Son,
should adopt men as sons, and that the Holy Spirit, as
Spirit, should sanctify them, and that the Father should
justify him that receives sanctification, in order that the
name of the three Persons may be known in one essence.[1]
The Apostle was instructed in this opinion by the Gospel,
where it says, "Go and make disciples of all the nations,
baptising them in the name of the Father and of the
Son and of the Holy Ghost" (Matt. xxviii. 19), and so
he welcomes at the laver of baptism the name of the
Trinity, saying, "But ye were washed, but ye were
sanctified, but ye were justified in the name of our
Lord Jesus Christ and in the Spirit of our God."

[If men ever use the gift as an opportunity for sinning,
it is not the fault of Him who gives the grace, any
more than it is the fault of one who gives a dinner, if
the guests get drunk at it. You speak of men afterwards
going on still in their evil ways; but if they do, they cut
themselves off from the blessings which their baptism

---

[1] This is the seemingly Post-Nicene phrase which has inclined so
many critics to assign a late date to Macarius. But see Introd., p.
xviii. n. 3, and p. 155 n. 1. The theory that the passage is a later
interpolation is supported by the subject of the next objection.
Could Macarius have chosen anything more unfortunate than the
Three Persons to lead on to a defence of the Monarchy of God?

BOOK IV. xxv, xx, xxvi 143

has brought, and receive no pity, but cause harm to themselves by their very treatment of the gift.]

CHAPTER XX. Objection based on the Monarchy of God.[1]

But let us make a thorough investigation concerning the single rule[2] of the only God and the manifold rule of those who are worshipped as gods. You do not know how to expound the doctrine even of the single rule. For a monarch is not one who is alone in his existence, but who is alone in his rule. Clearly he rules over those who are his fellow-tribesmen, men like himself, just as the Emperor Hadrian was a monarch, not because he existed alone, nor because he ruled over oxen and sheep (over which herdsmen or shepherds rule), but because he ruled over men who shared his race and possessed the same nature. Likewise God would not properly be called a monarch, unless He ruled over other gods; for this would befit His divine greatness and His heavenly and abundant honour.

CHAPTER XXVI. Answer to objection based on the Monarchy of God.

[As you have taken an image to express the rule of one God over many, the first point in my answer must be the matter of similarity in name.[3] It is quite wrong to suppose that because things bear the same name they must be identical in reality. For example, the name

[1] This objection and the next, and also the answers contained in chapters xxvi., xxvii., and xxviii. are quoted by Nicephorus, in his *Antirrhetica*, and are to be found in D. Pitra's *Spicil. Solesm.* t. I. p. 309 et seq. See Introd., pp. x, xi, xxvii.
One interest of Nicephorus lies in the difference of his text from the Athens MS. The most notable in this chapter occurs in the first sentence, where he omits the words τοῦ μόνου θεοῦ καὶ τῆς πολυαρχίας.

[2] The word Monarchia (μοναρχία) seems to require translating thus, in order to bring it into contrast with the Polyarchia (πολυαρχία) which follows.

[3] ἐξ εἰκόνος ἡμῖν . . . τὸν λόγον κρατύνειν ἐσπούδασας. The mention of an "image" at the beginning of this answer may possibly have attracted the attention of Nicephorus to the passage. For it is on the question of image worship that he introduces it as supporting his own attitude.

of "warm" is given both to the fire and to the man who is warmed by it, but it is only the fire that is so by nature. He who has warmed himself is also warm, but only relatively.[1] So God alone is a god absolutely; the others are only such relatively,[2] although the name of "God" may be given to "gods many and lords many." God rules not as having the same name as other gods and therefore as one of them, but as supreme, and without being one of them. He is uncreate, and they are creatures, whom He has made, and it is thus that He rules over them. He does not grudge them the name of god if they simply draw their divinity from nearness to Him; it is when they turn away from Him that they fall into darkness.

The case of Hadrian is not a parallel, for as man he cannot be master of his fellow-men (who are like himself), but only as having the added power of tyrant. But God's is not a tyrannical rule over those who are like Himself, but a loving rule over His inferiors.

We may liken Him to the sun, which gives things light and beauty till they themselves are bright, and yet receives nothing back from them. Just so God makes the angels shine with a reflected Godhead, though they have no part in His actual deity.

And so the right thing to do is to worship Him who s God absolutely. To worship one who is merely such relatively is as great a mistake as to hope to get heat and light from a red-hot iron instead of from the fire itself, for the metal will soon resume its own nature. Such is the case of the man who worships an angel or any other spiritual being except the one true God.

As the sun gives light to all, and yet loses none, and as the teacher imparts his teaching and yet retains his wisdom, so does God give all things and yet lack none, and so did power go out from Christ to heal the sick, and yet it remained within Him.]

---

[1] The same illustration is used in ii. 9.

[2] θέσει, in contrast with φύσει, philosophic terms by which he expresses his argument. Literally, "by position" and "by nature." See ii. 9.

CHAPTER XXI. Objection based on the immortal angels (Matt. xxii. 29–30), and the finger of God, with which He wrote on the tables of stone (Exod. xxxi. 18).

At any rate, if you say that angels stand before God, who are not subject to feeling and death, and immortal in their nature, whom we ourselves speak of as gods, because they are close to the Godhead, why do we dispute about a name? And are we to consider it only a difference of nomenclature?[1] For she who is called by the Greeks Athene is called by the Romans Minerva; and the Egyptians, Syrians, and Thracians address her by some other name. But I suppose nothing in the invocation of the goddess is changed or lost by the difference of the names. The difference therefore is not great, whether a man calls them gods or angels, since their divine nature bears witness to them, as when Matthew writes thus: "And Jesus answered and said, Ye do err, not knowing the scriptures, nor the power of God; for in the resurrection they neither marry nor are given in marriage, but are as the angels in heaven" (Matt. xxii. 29–30). Since therefore He confesses that the angels have a share in the divine nature,[2] those who make a suitable object of reverence for the gods, do not think that the god[3] is in the wood or stone or bronze from which the image is manufactured, nor do they consider that, if any part of the statue is cut off, it detracts from the power of the god. For the images of living creatures and the temples were set up by the ancients for the sake of remembrance, in order that those who approach thither might come to the knowledge of the god when they go; or, that, as they

[1] These first sentences are placed by Nicephorus under the objection of the previous chapter. It is to be noted that the matter of naming was mentioned there, and answered by Macarius, whereas his answer to this question is silent on this point. It is therefore possible that Nicephorus preserves the right order.

[2] An ancient reader was unable to restrain himself, and wrote in the margin of the MS., "This is not true."

[3] Blondel gives Θεός, not θεός, in this passage.

observe a special time and purify themselves generally,[1] they may make use of prayers and supplications, asking from them the things of which each has need. For if a man makes an image of a friend, of course he does not think that the friend is in it, or that the limbs of his body are included in the various parts of the representation; but honour is shown towards the friend by means of the image. But in the case of the sacrifices that are brought to the gods, these are not so much a bringing of honour to them as a proof of the inclination of the worshippers, to show that they are not without a sense of gratitude. It is reasonable that the form of the statues should be the fashion of a man, since man is reckoned to be the fairest of living creatures and an image of God. It is possible to get hold of this doctrine from another saying, which asserts positively that God has fingers, with which He writes, saying, "And he gave to Moses the two tables which were written by the finger of God" (Exod. xxxi. 18). Moreover, the Christians also, imitating the erection of the temples, build very large houses,[2] into which they go together and pray, although there is nothing to prevent them from doing this in their own houses, since the Lord[3] certainly hears from every place.

---

[1] There may be something wrong about τὸ λοιπὸν καθαρεύοντας. Nicephorus reads τῶν λοιπῶν.

[2] This statement has been taken as proof that the author wrote after the beginning of the new encouragement of Christianity shown by Constantine. For during the period that it was an unlawful religion (till A.D. 312), there were not the larger churches, which began to be built immediately afterwards. But the force of the argument is weakened by the many reasons there are for believing that the philosopher's date is earlier.

[3] τοῦ κυρίου is an addition by Nicephorus. It scarcely sounds like the language of the objector, but a subject of some sort is wanted.

CHAPTER XXVII. Answer to the objection based on the immortal angels (Matt. xxii. 29-30), and the finger of God, with which He wrote on the tables of stone (Exod. xxxi. 18).

Further, we will state the proposition in due measure concerning the angels and their immortality, and how in the kingdom of heaven "they neither marry nor are given in marriage, but are as angels in heaven." Christ, wishing to show the blessedness of those who have been granted to dwell in the heavenly place, and the misfortune of those who dwell amid the corruption of the earth, and have received their condition through the unclean growth of the flesh, being begotten and begetting and departing quickly like leaves, conveys the following meaning: "Those who have been thought worthy to enter into a life which knows no destruction, embark on a course which is worthy of kings, and is such as the angels have. They are rid of physical union, they no longer experience death, nor even birth, and are shut off from earthly embraces and bonds." He said this in order that any man who was well disposed, on hearing of a rational existence in heaven, which is associated with the Word of immortality, might adapt his life to the imitation of them,[1] and in his deeds would zealously affect their merit, refraining from marriage and fleeing from the symbols of corruption. And in the end he would pass through the door of death, and rise, with earthly weights removed, to the hall of the blessed, that is, of the angels. He does not however represent them by fashioning images of them,[2] as you yourself declare, nor does he speak to

---

[1] Blondel's edition follows Nicephorus in reading αὐτῶν, and prints λόγῳ earlier in the sentence, and not Λόγῳ. The MS. reads αὐτῷ, which would refer to "the Word." As here translated, αὐτῶν, and also ἐκείνων in the following clause, of course refer to the angels.

[2] Nicephorus is answering the Iconoclastic party, who were utterly opposed to the use of Christian images. They had garbled the words of Macarius to suit their purpose, taking the words οὐ μὴν εἰκόνας ἐκείνων τυπώσας τῷ σχήματι κ.τ.λ., and referring them

what is a shadow and rejoice in that which his imagination has created, associating with things soulless and material as if they were possessed of life, delighting in dead visions of forms, bringing his supplication to a dumb thing which he has moulded, deciding that the divine lurks in stone and wood, imagining that such matter as cannot be held at all, is held by bronze and iron, and picturing in a dead vision and without any sense that he is catching that which cannot be caught.[1]

And again, if it be true that angels have sometimes appeared in human form, yet they were not really that which appeared, but that which they were was invisible. And if any one fashions a picture or a representation in bronze, he does not make that which it really is, nor does he enclose its nature therein.

[As for God being so material as to have "fingers," etc., Scripture does not mean that He can be divided into limbs and parts of a body. This is not meant to refer to His nature, but He is thus spoken of in order that men may understand. To suppose that God has material fingers and other parts because man must conceive of Him thus, is no more true than that it is a real lion that a man has seen when he has beheld one in a dream. Similarly the angels who appeared to Abraham were not really of the human form and behaviour they appeared to be, as is sufficiently proved by the way they consumed the food offered them. So Abraham made no image of them, except in the mindful tablets of his mind.]

---

to *Christian* images, and omitting the words just before them. Nicephorus (*op. cit.* p. 322) shows that Macarius is only speaking from the Greek point of view, as the words ὡς φῂς αὐτός prove, and that he would not be answering his opponent if they referred to Christian images.

[1] θηρᾶν τὸ ἀθήρατον. This is more likely than the ἀθέατον of the text of Nicephorus, showing that the latter is only occasionally a guide to the true reading.

CHAPTER XXII. Objection based on the Incarnation of the Word.

But even supposing any one of the Greeks were so light-minded as to think that the gods dwell within the statues, his idea would be a much purer one than that of the man who believes that the Divine entered into the womb of the Virgin Mary, and became her unborn child, before being born and swaddled in due course, for it is a place full of blood and gall, and things more unseemly still.

CHAPTER XXVIII. Answer to the objection based on the Incarnation of the Word.

If it seems to you far preferable that the Divine should be pleased to dwell in a statue, and not have been made flesh in Mary on account of the humiliation of such an experience, listen more fully to the mystery of the doctrine, how that the all-sufficient and creative Word, though He be great and powerful and far removed from feeling, yet has not feared to face all the things that are a cause of shame among ourselves. For He is without feeling in that wherein He is not ashamed to be born like men who are subject to feeling. He is without defilement in that wherein He receives no corruption through wickedness. Therefore the Word is made flesh, not lowering Himself to the disease or humiliation of the flesh, but leading the things of the flesh to His own immortality. For just as the sun when it descends into wetness does not receive a sense of wetness, and is not found to be muddy, but dries up the wetness of the mud, keeping the water away from itself altogether, and not having its rays affected, even so God the Word, who is the Sun of the world of mind, though descending to the flesh, draws up no sickness therefrom, and is not found either overcome by its passions or falling by reason of the weakness of its evil nature. On the contrary, by leading it up from its slippery places, and dragging it up out of its misfortunes, He set it in a divine blessedness that was allotted to it, giving it warmth when it was wasting away, and holding it together when it was being dissolved by its sins. The result was to make it irresistible and invincible and able to conquer the assaults of its defects, so that the flesh might retain its nature and yet disown the accusation which that nature involves, preserving its limits and yet rejecting the confusion which those limits cause. This is the reason that He worked out the fulfilment of the dispensation, not in any other thing, but in the flesh. Nor did He do this in flesh of any unique kind, but in human flesh, and moreover in that of a virgin. This was in order that He might show that it was from the virgin earth that He took the flesh and made it in the beginning, as the dwelling-place of mind and reason and soul, and in like manner He now prepared a temple for Himself from a maid and virgin, without needing the hand and art of man. Pray, which is the more precious of the two—soil, or a virgin? Man or mud? Surely man is superior to mud, and a virgin more precious than soil. If, therefore, God is not ashamed to take soil from the earth, but works in muddy material and fashions man from it, how will He delay to take man from man, or how will He hesitate to wear flesh from a virgin? Will He not set aside all lingering and delay, and take hold of that compound which is more precious than the earth, and make from it an image that bears His Godhead, in the birth of the Only-begotten?[1] It is as dwelling in this image that He shakes the world by the beauty of His virtue, and flashes light upon all by the grace of His gift.

Prometheus, whose story is well known among yourselves, fashions man, and there is no shame at all about it. And Zeus makes in Athena a woman who came to life, and you approve of the myth and magnify the fact, without seeing anything shameful in it or reckoning it a

[1] θεοφόρον ἄγαλμα μονογενῶς ἐργάσεται. If μονογενῶς is not to be connected with the name which the author uses as the sub-title of his book, it may only mean "by an unique birth." Could it mean "by a birth that is single"?

misfortune, and not enquiring into the question of hidden parts. And yet, if there is really any shame about it at all, it is much more shameful to fashion parts and conceal them with certain coverings, than to pass through them for the sake of the dispensation and the word that brings profit.[1] For he who makes a building and then turns round and refuses to live in it, stands self-accused, and is an implacable judge of himself, because he did not reckon that there was any question of shame when he was making it; but after its completion, he slanders the result of his own labours, by judging the work on which he has lavished his care to be unfit to dwell in. So the Deity, in making man, incurs the charge of injustice, if He is ashamed to dwell in him, and refuses to take His portion from him. For by so doing He has made the workmanship of His own exertion to be of no value at all, and has slandered all His own wisdom by ignoring it, because He made a representation of His own glory, and then decided that it was shameful to dwell in it.

CHAPTER XXIII. Objection based on the saying: "Thou shalt not revile gods" (Exod. xxii. 28).

I could also give proof to you of that insidious name of "gods" from the law, when it cries out and admonishes the hearer with much reverence, "Thou shalt not revile gods, and thou shalt not speak evil of the ruler of thy people." For it does not speak to us of other gods than those already within our reckoning, from what we know in the words, "Thou shalt not go after gods" (Jer. vii. 6); and again, "If ye go and worship other gods" (Deut. xii. 28). It is not men, but the gods who are held in honour by us, that are meant, not only by Moses, but by his successor Joshua. For he says to the people, "And now fear him and serve him alone, and put away the gods whom your fathers served" (Josh. xxiv. 14). And it is not concerning men,

[1] The passage beginning with the mention of Prometheus and ending here, is quoted by Nicephorus, *Antirrhet.*, *loc. cit.*

but incorporeal beings that Paul says, "For though there be that are called gods, whether on earth or in heaven, yet to us there is but one God and Father, of whom are all things" (1 Cor. viii. 5). Therefore you make a great mistake in thinking that God is angry if any other is called a god, and obtains the same title as Himself. For even rulers do not object to the title from their subjects,[1] nor masters from slaves. And it is not right to think that God is more petty-minded than men. Enough then about the fact that Gods exist, and ought to receive honour.

CHAPTER XXIX. Answer to the objection based on the saying: "Thou shalt not revile gods" (Exod. xxii. 28).

[So we must be afraid to hold such an opinion, but we must confess that God took our flesh, and not think of Him as dwelling in statues.[2] Nor must we call the four elements gods, nor deify the stars, even though the name of their motion may suggest it.[3] It is the charioteer and not the horses that receives the crown of victory, and the honour must be all for God who guides the stars. Even though statues were actually to talk, we must not give them honour. The words of Moses, "Thou shalt not revile gods," are spoke of men, not gods. What he means is that those may be called "gods" to whom the word of God has come, just as those are called warm whom the fire has warmed.[4] It is only men's folly that has imagined God to be in images. Moses does not mean supernatural gods in this sense, for no one would uselessly revile such a god, which had no consciousness whereby to perceive his abuse. The Deity is no more interfered

---

[1] He means that even men sometimes have the title. He might have quoted, as our Lord did, "I said, ye are gods" (John x. 34). If it can be used by men concerning each other, it can be used of higher beings.

[2] He here continues the thoughts of his last chapter.

[3] There is a play on words here; the stars run (θέωσιν) but are not θεοί in consequence (τούτους μὴ θειάσωμεν).

[4] See chapter xxvi. *init.*

with by men bearing His name, than a man would be by a dog being called after him. To call mean things "gods" does God Himself no harm, it is only mocking the name. God is not angry at it, but it only brings harm on those who do it.]

CHAPTER XXIV. Objection based on the resurrection of the flesh.[1]

Let us once again discuss the question of the resurrection of the dead. For what is the reason that God should act thus, and upset in this random way the succession of events that has held good until now, whereby He ordained that races should be preserved and not come to an end, though from the beginning He has laid down these laws and framed things thus? The things which have once been determined by God, and preserved through such long ages, ought to be everlasting, and ought not to be condemned by Him who wrought them, and destroyed as if they had been made by some mere man, and arranged as mortal things by one who is himself a mortal. Wherefore it is ridiculous if, when the whole is destroyed, the resurrection shall follow, and if He shall raise—shall we say?—the man who died three years before the resurrection, and along with him Priam and Nestor who died a thousand years before, and others who lived before them from the beginning of the human race. And if any one is prepared to grasp even this, he will find that the question of the resurrection is one full of silliness. For many have often perished in the sea, and their bodies have been consumed by fishes, while many have been eaten by wild beasts and birds. How then is it possible for their bodies to rise up? Come then, and let us put to the test this statement which is so lightly made. Let us take an example. A man was shipwrecked, the

[1] The title of the chapter uses the phrase, so familiar in early creeds, "Resurrectio carnis." And although his opponent calls it "the resurrection of the dead," the former phrase is used in his answer as well as in the title of it.

mullets devoured his body, next these were caught and eaten by some fishermen, who were killed and devoured by dogs; when the dogs died ravens and vultures feasted on them and entirely consumed them. How then will the body of the shipwrecked man be brought together, seeing that it was absorbed by so many creatures? Again, suppose another body to have been consumed by fire, and another to have come in the end to the worms, how is it possible for it to return to the essence [1] which was there from the beginning?

You will tell me that this is possible with God, but this is not true. For all things are not possible with Him; He simply cannot bring it about that Homer should not have become a poet, or that Troy should not be taken. Nor indeed can He make twice two, which make the number four, to be reckoned as a hundred, even though this may seem good to Him. Nor can God ever become evil, even though He wishes; nor would He be able to sin, as being good by nature. If then He is unable to sin or to become evil, this does not befall Him through His weakness. In the case of those who have a disposition and fitness for a certain thing, and then are prevented from doing it, it is clear that it is by their weakness that they are prevented. But God is by nature good, and is not prevented from being evil; nevertheless, even though He is not prevented, he cannot become bad.

And pray consider a further point. How unreasonable it is if the Creator shall stand by and see the heaven melting, though no one ever conceived anything more wonderful than its beauty, and the stars falling, and the earth perishing; and yet He will raise up the rotten and corrupt bodies of men, some of them, it is true, belonging to admirable men, but others without charm or symmetry before they died, and affording a most unpleasant sight. Again, even if He could easily make them rise in a comely form, it would be impossible for the earth to hold all those who had died from the beginning of the world, if they were to rise again.

[1] ὑπόστασις.

CHAPTER XXX. Answer to the objection based on the resurrection of the flesh.

[Do not raise an uproar against me, for there is no doubt that the resurrection is a difficulty. I will speak simply, and not with any flowery language which might deceive, like a base coin washed over with gold.]

First of all we may fitly consider the following point : has that which is created come into being from what existed already or not ? If it was from what had an existence, there was no sense in attaching a beginning to it. But if such a beginning has to be attached, the reason is quite plain (*i.e.* that it was made from nothing). But if, from being nothing, God has given it an existence, what kind of essence[1] did He grant to that which had none just before? For He who brought into being that which was not, will be all the more likely to preserve that which came into existence, even when it is dissolved, and to think it deserving of a better conclusion to be added. For it is the property of a nature that is unbegotten to change for the better the existence of the things that are begotten, and to lead to a renewal the things which He has created in time, and to wipe off with grace the things which were stained with the poison of wickedness, and to consider the things which were exhausted as worthy of a second beginning and a kind of remaking. For the world, after again receiving a better form and covering, does not dissolve its being, but on the contrary, it rejoices in being clothed with a fairer beauty than that which it received before. It befits the Divine alone to remain in a state of sameness, but for creation it is suitable that it should suffer change and alteration. Therefore the present life and order is our guide, leading us like children to the future assembly of immortality, and preparing us to face the glory that will lead us upward. For our present life is like a womb con-

[1] Reading τίνα for τίς (ὑπόστασιν ἐχαρίσατο;). This passage is an example of the fact that Macarius does not ordinarily use this word as meaning "person." See Introd., p. xviii, and p. 142 n. 1.

taining a babe, for it holds down the whole being of things in obscurity, in the forgetfulness of ignorance, where the light does not penetrate. The whole of what is growing must rise from the present age as from the membrane which holds it in the womb, and must receive a second mode of life in the light of the abiding place which is inviolable.

You would like to think that corruption goes on without end, that it is born in foulness and dies in filth, that it begets and is begotten and is covered in forgetfulness, that evil flourishes and calamity increases, that it melts through want and grows thin through poverty, suffering ill by day and sleeping by night, eating in luxury and then again in bitterness weighed down with satiety, and suffering in scarcity; a state alike of slavery and mastership, the rich man standing up and the poor man lying down, the old man falling and the young man rising, the breasts of women growing and the babe receiving suck, sorrow being brought by care and disease by toil, the life of the country hated and the life of the city welcomed, equality being shunned and that which is unequal being sought after, the nature of things troubled by much anomaly, cast down in winter and burning in summer, brightened by the flowers of spring in their season, and nourished by the fruits of autumn, digging the earth and working its clods . . . making a tragedy of existence and a comedy of life. . . . And that the hateful covering of these things should never pass away, even late in time, nor their dark robe disappear; that the soul should never be free from the inhuman earth; that lamentation should never be silent; . . . that the violence of tyrants should never die; . . . that the toil of those that groan should never be lightened, nor the tears of the mourners comforted; that the virtues of those who have mastered themselves should never shine forth, nor the boasting of the proud be quenched; that the deeds of the unrighteous should never be punished, nor the success of the righteous be seen; that there should be no judgment of the cunning of quackery and no honour for the guilelessness of the sincere; . . . that the earth should

BOOK IV. xxx

never be freed from pollutions,[1] nor the sea have rest from navigation ;[2] that the world should not be turned round like a wheel and preserve its essence while changing its form; that everything in the whole world should not receive a renewal apart from the things which transcend it, nor receive a genuine newness of life ; that the order of things should never put off its disorder, nor cast aside the unseemliness which it has now, but retain its grievous garb beyond the limits of time, and be yet more exhausted by its calamities !

For that which appears to be brought down upon the world as wholly a ruin and a destruction is really the beginning of immortality and the starting-point of salvation. For a second beautifying of life will make it a success, when rational nature shall a second time receive in the resurrection the word of a beginning which will be indissoluble. It is for the sake of man that the whole suffers change, seeing that it was also for his sake that at the outset it was deemed worthy of a beginning. Man was made on his own account, not on account of any other being, but heaven and earth and the things that appertain to them are created on man's account, and when he receives a change and alteration, the whole must be changed and wiped out along with him. Think of an architect who builds a house to begin with, and then when it has grown weak in course of time and come to an end by a fall, he raises it up again and considers it worthy of better workmanship and comeliness, not troubling himself which stone was laid first in the beginning or which was second or third in the building ; but he erects it by setting in the last stones among the first and the first among the last, and the middle ones haphazard, not in the least disturbing the plan of the erection thereby, nor causing the arrangement of his workmanship to be found fault with; but, by applying suitable adornment to the house and decorating the form of its appearance, he receives abundant praise

[1] μιασμάτων—perhaps in the sense of "noxious mists."
[2] An unexpected word ; perhaps it should be ναυαγίας, "shipwreck."

for his skill. Just in the same way God became the maker of reasoning beings like an architect making a house, and created man in the beginning, and built him as the sacred abode of divine power, composed of many kindred races like stones. And after he has been made for many ages and seasons, and has fallen by many experiences of sins, and in the end is altogether undone and destroyed, He will raise him up again, and will bring nature together with skilful understanding and wise authority, and will gather together the things that have been scattered, allowing none of the things that have fallen to perish; and, even though He place the first among the last in His arrangement, and bring those at the end into the first rank of merit, He will not at all disturb what He has done, but will grant that setting forth of the resurrection which is suitable to each.

And even if it is as you say, and Priam or Nestor died a thousand years ago, while some other man may die three days before the resurrection, none of them when he rises again will feel either measureless grief or abundance of joy therefrom, but each of them will receive what is suitable to him in accordance with his own deeds, and he will not have either blame or praise for the arrangement of the resurrection, neither for its speediness nor again for its tardiness, but it will be his own manner of life that he will either delight in or find fault with. For with God a period of a thousand years is reckoned as one brief day (cf. 2 Peter iii. 8),[1] and again the brief space, if He thinks fit, becomes the stretching out of countless ages. Therefore these are the words of petty folk, when they say, "If He is going to raise up the man who died three days before in like manner as the man of a thousand years before, He does a very great injustice."

[For in ancient times men lived to be five hundred or more, and the man who died just before the resurrection may have had a sorry life and not lived to be thirty. It is doubtless in accordance with a divine plan that the

---

[1] See p. 125, n. 3.

BOOK IV. xxx

former should sleep the longest, and the latter should receive speedier consolation.

As for your childish objection based on the shipwrecked man who was eaten by fishes and they by men, the men by dogs, and the dogs by vultures, making it impossible for his resurrection to take place, your words are like those of a man dreaming in a drunken sleep.]

For you suggest that He who makes the fire would not have the power to work in the way that fire does, in bringing about the resurrection. For when there is silver and gold lying in the soil, or lead and tin, bronze and iron, as it were hidden away somewhere, fire, by burning the soil and heating the material, brings out the silver and gold, etc., so as to separate them, allowing none of their essence to perish, unless there is something earthy in them anywhere which admits of destruction. If then the power of fire is so strong and has such a drastic effect that it brings out pure material from some other material, and preserves the essence of each undestroyed, even though the gold has fallen into countless cavities, and is dissolved into endless fragments and scattered into mire or clay, in heaps of earth or of dung; and if the fire, when applied to all, preserves the gold and expels the substance of the parts that are destructible, what are we to say about Him who ordained the nature of the fire? Pray would He not have the power without even an effort to change man, His rational treasure more precious than gold, who is contained in matter of various kinds, and to set before Him safe and sound those who have perished by land or sea, in rivers or in lakes, those who have been eaten by wild beasts or birds, those who have been dissolved into fine dust that cannot be measured? Will He be found to be less effective than the fire? And will He be impotent by the arguments you have adduced?

As for that strange phantasy which has come into your head, that God cannot do all things, you think to shape it into plausibility by means of your arguments, but it is really like a prop without foundation, and does not stand. How shall we make it clear to you that God has power to do all things? Shall it be from the divine essence itself, or from the sense of fitness? Or shall we test the question from both of the two, and expound to you first, if that is what you like, the meaning of the point at issue as judged from the inviolable nature itself? For instance, if God is able to make that which has been made to be not made, that which is created necessarily changes into that which is uncreated. But if we grant this, it follows that we may argue that there are two uncreated things; or rather, nothing is created, but the whole is uncreated. From such reasoning much that is fabulous results, for in this way even that which is uncreated will be created. But when that which is uncreated comes under the head of the created, the argument about the created does not stand. For who will be the maker of the created, if the uncreated does not exist?

Akin to this is the question whether God, who is uncreated, can make Himself created. As some say that it is impossible for the uncreated to become created, He cannot do so. And since He is righteous, He will grant justice by avenging the downtrodden. For if He were not to do this, His power would manifestly be nothing but slackness and folly, that He should make all things and penetrate them by a law of creation, and then that He should despise them, giving no honour to that which welcomed virtue in this life, and no judgment to that which gave heed to wickedness during the course of existence; but that He should allow that which is good and its opposite to be plunged alike in forgetfulness, neither crowning the virtue as virtue nor laying bare the wickedness, . . . but simply allowing human nature to be tossed about in silence, as though it had no existence, and making no investigation of either the wickedness in it or the virtue. Such a belief as this does not suit with the divine providence, nor does this idea accord with the immortal nature. On the contrary, it is altogether different, and quite strange and foreign to the attitude of Him who is inviolable[1] and far removed from it, that God should thus have no care for the things of His own creation, standing by and watching the destruction of the theory of His creative workmanship, and paying no heed when men depart into obscurity.

We conclude therefore that He will raise up all things, and will grant them a second existence. He will judge the world for the things wherein it has sinned, sparing those who have believed in Him sincerely, and punishing those who were not willing to receive Him, nor reverencing the mystery of His appearing. All the colts that are signed with the king's letter and mark are deemed worthy of a royal stable and manger; and even though they be feeble in body and ineffective in strength and sluggish in running, and though they be not like the rest in condition, yet because of that which is marked on them[2] they are precious and honourable. But all those that have not the royal branding, even though they may be nimble and swift, and impossible to overtake, and though they be of good racing ancestry, and of high renown, are nevertheless expelled from the royal stables (and this illustration is not a myth or the narrative of a story-teller, but a genuine record, and a true relation of known facts). Just in the same way all who were sealed with the sign of salvation, who engraved the almighty Name on the tablet of their soul, all who judged their confession towards God more potent than their own sins, these have escaped the danger of the judgment to come, and sailed without harm past what may be called Charybdis, gazing with the eye of faith on the common light of their salvation and the abundant redemption of Him who came to earth. For as the man who had put on a breastplate strong and thick and that cannot be loosed from his shoulders, is unwounded in war, and is not taken prisoner when terrors stand round about him, even so the man who has put on the confession of Him who is mightier than he, has no fear of the threatening of universal judgment. For as the fire does not consume

[1] τῆς ἀχράντου περιωπῆς. [2] διὰ τὸν χαρακτῆρα.

that which is called "inviolable,"[1] and does not burn the sword but brightens and tempers it, so those who are dipped in the inviolable Name will never be affected by fire or by judgment, which will flee before the Name which is named upon them.

If a man has an eye that is able to see, the sun fills it with abundant light when it is opened, but when the eye is shut it commits it to darkness. The sun itself does nothing wrong, and does not harm his vision; but the man who is possessed of sight has brought his own penalty. He is not wronged by the sun's rays, but he made darkness for himself out of those things in which he might have shown himself to be co-operating with the light, by receiving a proof of light in his seeing the sun, and by having a proof of darkness in his not seeing it, he himself being in both cases his own arbiter and judge. Even thus a man who believes in God and trusts in Him, who may be termed the divine light of the mind, is found to be a partner of God in whom he believes, shunning the darkness of ignorance and want of knowledge, and nourished by the brightness of heavenly doctrines, being himself aware of salvation beforehand through beholding the divine, and having in his own possession, as a great and sufficient preservation of his faith, the remedy of salvation. But the man who is disabled by the blindness of wilful unbelief, and, turning away from the brightness of the light in which all may share, moves in the darkness like some creature swimming in the depths of the sea, showing no fulfilment of the good deeds of virtue, receives no praise even though he be wise apart from the light. And even though he co-operate with those who are near him, he receives no dignity; and even if he does what is righteous but does not take the light as test and judge, his labours are subject to blame, and he does not escape from accusation. And even though his soul be trained in natural righteousness, hating plunder and refraining from theft, not breaking through the rights of other men's marriages, not despising or insulting his neigh-

[1] ἀμίαντον. It cannot be translated asbestos, as it is repeated in the ἀμίαντον ὄνομα of the next clause.

bour, but fighting for his fatherland, enduring ills on behalf of his kindred, and showing all kinds of excellences in his deeds, he is without sanctification and does everything to no purpose, since he does not accept the mastership of Him who perishes not, as the judge of all that is done by him.

For as beauty has no praise apart from the beauty of the light, and a reckoning does not receive its completion apart from the measuring rule of the things that are measured, even so right action and all the virtue and ordering of men's deeds, when it does not accept as test and judge the unsleeping eye of that gaze which beholds all things, is like a pearl hidden in the mud, the beauty of which is not seen in the light but is concealed in a rubbish heap.[1] For tell me, who will crown or reward the restraint of the man who has self-control? Who will honour the soldier with pay after his deed of valour? Who will deem worthy of rewards the man who has contended in the games? Is not his running, merely considered in itself, a matter of blame? Is not the success of the man who has done his soldiering to no purpose apart from his general? Is not the contest of him who has the mastery of himself a pitiable thing without one to crown him? Is not the tribute of subjects of no benefit without a king? Even thus the issue of every kind of righteousness is stripped of the reward of the good, if it be not done in the name and to the honour of the Creator. And, on the other hand, any man who believes that there is One who is potent to behold and judge his deeds and activities, even though he be full of guilt, and the servant of unholy practices, and though he have set himself to be a follower of abominable deeds, by bringing the examination of his own deeds before the eyes of the Creator (just as the sick man discloses the affections of his body to a sympathetic physician), he is freed from all grief and trouble, and is rid of the countless stripes of his transgressions. For the Saviour is able to sa— . . .

(Here the Athens MS. ends.)

[1] There appears to be an intentional alliteration in οὐκ ἐν φωτί, ἀλλ' ἐν φορυτῷ.

BOOK V

[Fragment quoted in Greek by F. Turrianus (De la Torre), *Dogmaticus de Justificatione, ad Germanos adversus Luteranos*, Romae, 1557, p. 37.][1]

The subject is Faith and Works, and Turrianus says that Magnetes writes as follows concerning the faith of Abraham :—

For having believed through good works, he was well-pleasing to God, and therefore was considered worthy of the friendship of Him who is higher. By doing these things he caused his faith to shine brighter than the sun. And together with his faith he works what is right, wherefore he is beloved of God and honoured. For, knowing that faith is the foundation of success, he roots it deep, building upon it the multitude of mercies. For, joining each of the two things with a kindred bond, he raises on each a lofty rampart, by acquiring a faith which receives the testimony of works. Nor again does he allow the works to be base, or sundered from the faith, but knowing that faith is a seed which produces abundant fruit, he brings together all things that are brought in contact with the seed, earth, ploughman, wallet, yoke, plough, and as many things as the husbandman's skill has devised. For as the seed is not sown apart from these, and reason completes none of the things mentioned above apart from the seed, so faith which in some sense stands for mystical seed, is unfruitful if it abides alone, unless it grow by means of good works. And in like manner the linking together of good deeds is a useless thing and altogether incomplete, unless it have faith woven in with it. Wherefore, in order that it may reveal Abraham as

[1] This quotation also appears in Latin form in his *Adversus Magdaburgenses*, lib. iv. ch. 7.

BOOK V 165

making the grace of his works to shine forth from faith, the divine Scripture says, "Abraham believed God, and it was reckoned unto him for righteousness" (Gen. xv. 6).[1]

You see how faith made preceding good deeds of virtue to be reckoned for righteousness, just as the sowing makes the land to bring forth fruit.

For as a light makes the quality of the oil to shine forth when put in a lamp, so faith, being as it were put into a lamp, made the virtue of Abraham's works to give a brilliant light. For Abraham, as a natural result of his teaching, welcomed what was just and equal in social life, and showed himself serviceable to his neighbours, and without guile, living to avoid evil both in giving and in receiving, giving consolation without stint to those who needed it; in a word, he refrained from evil[2] practices. But even if these things were good in appearance and respected, yet no one reckoned them, no one set virtue under its right heading, for no one had the power to do so, save God only, and he did not yet believe. But when Abraham believed God, these things, experiences of this kind that were good, were reckoned unto Abraham for righteousness.

Turrianus ends the above quotation with the words "Hactenus Magnetes," but there are strong reasons for thinking that he is still reproducing the substance of the *Apocriticus* in the words that follow. (For the arguments which make this probable, see *J.T.S.* vol. viii. No. 32, July 1907, pp. 559–560.)

After referring to the above three parables of the building, the seed, and the lamp, he adds (in Latin):—

There is yet a fourth parable, and a very apt one, as it seems to me—namely, that of the lump and the leaven,

---

[1] τὸ προλαβὸν κατόρθωμα. Like the fragment of Book I., the language is here linked with that of the rest of Macarius by the use of his favourite word, which occurs three times in this fragment.

[2] Turrianus gives φάβλων, but his Latin rendering "pravis" shows it to have been φαύλων.

showing how faith is like the lump, while good and spiritual works are like leaven. For bread is unpleasant without leaven, and difficult for digestion and nutrition; and again, leaven alone without the lump is altogether useless, but when it is added to the lump it makes it pleasant and firm, wholesome and easy of digestion. Even so love, when we walk according to God's commands, is like leaven in binding and permeating the whole lump of faith, that is to say, by making it firm and fermenting it, it renders it wholesome and useful. Thus the lump of faith without the leaven of love and good works is neither useful nor a wholesome food for the soul, nor is it pleasing to God; nor again is love fitting, however wide it be, without the lump of faith. But it is the combination and mingling of the two that is wholesome. This new mixture of faith and good works is pleasing to God, without the old leaven, that is to say, without the corruption of concupiscence which is in the world.[1]

[1] It is uncertain what form of attack Macarius is here answering. It does not seem likely that he is simply dealing with the quotation from Genesis about Abraham's faith. And if the argument centres in the difference between the teaching of S. Paul and S. James on faith and works, it would be a return to the earlier objections of a detailed kind, whereas the latter part of Book IV. leads us to expect objections of a more general and doctrinal character. It would seem therefore as if Hierocles had gone on to attack the inner teachings of Christianity, and such difficulties within the faith as the reconciliation of justification by faith with the stress laid upon good works.

If this conclusion is correct, it shows us that the scope of the *Apocriticus* was wider than is supposed or its title would suggest, and the dialogue is seen to have had a much broader doctrinal range than the discussion of passages in the New Testament.

Internal evidence supports the genuineness of the fragment. The allegorical and Origenistic style of explanation is quite Macarian, and so is the language. His favourite word κατόρθωμα occurs no less than three times.

INDEX

allegory, xxii, 33, 48, 59, 67, 75, 81, 86, 89, 107, 108, 122, 132, 135, 136
Amphilochius, xix
angels, 122, 123, 136, 144, 145–148
anthropomorphism, 148
Antichrists, 129
Antioch, xv, xxi, xxii, 33
Apocalypse of Peter, xxv, 129, 131
Apocriticus, xxiv
Apocryphal references, xxvi, 123 *n*. 1, 127
Apollonius of Tyana, xvi, xxi, 52, 55, 127
Apotactites, 115
Aratus, xxi, 135
Athens MS., x, xi, xii, xiv, xxiv, xxvii, xxviii

Babylon, 120
baptism, 86, 87, 115
barbarians, 40
Bardesanes, 128
Bel and the Dragon, 123
Berenice, xi, 31
bishops, 85–88
Blondel, xii

catechumen, 87, 97
celibacy, 32, 113–115
Cerinthus, 128
Christomachi, xviii
churches, 146
Cilician, xxi, 115, 128
clouds (as meaning angels), 122
Codex Bezae, xxvi, 38

Contra Celsum, xxvi
corn (of Eucharist), 83
creation (the purpose of), 131
Cyprian, 87

demons, 36, 62–68, 89, 109–113
devil, 90, 93
,, deception of the, xix, xxvii, 58, 59
,, father of the, 49, 50
,, as slanderer, 48, 50
Docetism, xxix, 56
Dositheus, xxi, 115, 128
Droserius, 128
Duchesne, xii, xiv, xv, xxvii

Edessa, xi, xiii, xv, xxi, 31, 128
Encratites, 115
Eremites, 115
Ethiopia, xxi, 79, 125
Eucharist, xxviii, xxix, 80–85
Eusebius, xvii, 31
Ezra, 60, 61

Fabian, 87
faith, 164–166
forgiveness, 140
Foucart, xii

Godhead (of Christ), 76, 77, 84
gods, 151–152
Gregory of Nyssa, xix, xxvii

Hadrian, 143, 144
Harnack, xiii–xv, xxii, xxiii, 51, 95, 111, 128
heaven, 130–133

INDEX

heretics, 114–116, 128
Herodotus, 41
Hierocles, xiii, xv–xvii, xxii, xxiv
history (writing of), 41
Holy Spirit, 96, 113, 118, 124, 141, 142
hypostasis (ὑπόστασις), xviii, 34, 64

Iconoclasts, 147
idols, 112
images, 112, 143–148
immortality, 157
Incarnation, 83, 113, 149

Jews, 40, 44, 45, 48, 49, 54, 66, 79, 103
judgment, 161, 163

keys of heaven, 94–98

Lactantius, xvi, xvii
lake, 64, 74
law of Moses, 103–108, 140, 152
leaven, 135, 166
legion, 67
Logos, 132

Macarius, name and authorship, xix, xx
,, Homilies on Genesis, xiv
Macrobians, 79, 125
Magnus Crusius, xii
Manes, 128
Manichæans, 115, 129
Marcion, 128
martyrdom, 127
Mary Magdalene, 43
Maurusians, 125
monarchy (of God), xviii, 128
monasticism, 33
Monogenes, xiv, xix, xxiv, 33, 55, 60, 77, 106
Montanus, xxi, 128
mountains (in allegorical sense), 89

Neumann, xxiv
Nicephorus, x, xi, xx, xxix, 31, 143, 147

Oracles, 110, 111
Origen, xiii, xiv, xix, xxii, xxvi, xxix
ousia (οὐσία), xviii, 34, 64, 132
oxen (God's care for), 104, 107

Palmyra, 120
parasang, xxi, 106
Passion, 53, 56, 58, 76, 77, 93
Paul, 99–116
,, (martyrdom of), xxvi, 126, 127 *n.* 1
Paul and Thecla, Acts of, xxiv, 32
Peter, 91–98
,, (as Rock-man), 93, 94
,, (his crucifixion), 126, 127 *n.* 1
,, Second Epistle, xxv, 125 *n.* 3, 158
,, Apocalypse of, xxv, 129, 131
Philalethes, xiii, xv, xvi, xxii, xxiv
physiological explanation of Sacraments, 82
Pilate, 44, 54, 66
Polycarp, xxi, xxiii, 86, 87
Porphyry, xii–xiv, xvi, xxii, 110, 111
prophecy, 53, 90, 129

resurrection, 153–163
rock (of Christ's foundation), 94
Romans, 40, 43, 66, 102, 103
Romé (play on word), 103
Rufinus, xiv

sacrifices (heathen), 110, 146
satrapy, 128
Schalkhausser, xiv, xxvi, xxviii
Sea of Galilee, 64, 73, 74
Simon Magus, 128
spiritual healing, 87
Synod of the Oak, xiii, xx

INDEX

Theosthenes, 51, 117
traditions : Paul's beheading, 127 n. 1
,, Peter's crucifixion, 126, 127 n. 1
,, Polycarp's prayers, 86, 87
Trinitarian doctrine, xviii, xxviii, 141, 142
Turrianus, **x, xii, xxviii**, 164

Venice MS., **xii, xxvii, xxviii**
Virgin Mary, 149
virginity, 32, 113, 114

wine (Eucharistic), 83
Wisdom, 81, 82
Word, 75, 133, 137, 149
works, 164-166

Zenobia, 120

www.ingramcontent.com/pod-product-compliance
Lightning Source LLC
Chambersburg PA
CBHW071430160426
43195CB00013B/1864